Winchester, Massachusetts

The Architectural Heritage of a Victorian Town

The Winchester
Historical Society
Winchester, Massachusetts

Acknowledgments

Staff

Project Coordinator: Ragnhild M. Bairnsfather
Executive Editor: Jane E. Robbins
Text Writer: Kevin Stevens
Editorial/Production: Jane E. Robbins, Schneider & Co.
Design/Production: Judith Arisman Design
Photography: Robert M. LaVallee
Art Editor/Photoessays: Jane E. Robbins
House Survey Writers: Ragnhild M. Bairnsfather, Andrew Eisenmann,
Margaret S. Harvey, William O'Connor, Marcia Wood
Tour Maps: Warburton K. VerPlanck, Virginia M. Sorenson
Research: Ragnhild M. Bairnsfather, Kevin Stevens
Reviewers: Susan Keats, Bradley C. Ross
Book Committee: Walter J. Farrell, Jr., Margaret S. Harvey, William O'Connor,
Bradley C. Ross, Frances B. VerPlanck

Major Funding

The Massachusetts Arts Lottery as administered by the Winchester Arts Lottery
Council
En Ka Society
Arthur G. B. Metcalf Foundation
The Boslego Corporation

Photo and Art Credits

Except where otherwise noted, the old photographs in this book are from the H. E.
Simonds Memorial Archival Center, Winchester, Massachusetts.
The house style drawings and map locator inset were researched and prepared by Anne
E. Hritzay.

Library of Congress Cataloging-in-Publication Data

Winchester, Massachusetts : the architectural heritage of a Victorian town.

Bibliography: p.
1. Architecture, Victorian—Massachusetts—Winchester.   2. Architecture—
Massachusetts—Winchester.   3. Architecture, Domestic—Massachusetts—Winchester.
4. Winchester (Mass.)—Buildings, structures, etc.   5. Winchester (Mass.)—History.
I. Winchester Historical Society (Winchester, Mass.)   II. Title.
NA735.W537S7 1988   720'.9744'4   86–51623
First Edition
ISBN 0-9620357-0-X

Contents

Foreword

The National Historic Preservation Act of 1966 provides funds to state historic commissions throughout the United States for identifying and protecting their significant districts, buildings, sites, and structures. In 1976 the Winchester Historical Commission received a matching grant from the Massachusetts Historical Commission to identify and catalog Winchester's architectural heritage through a comprehensive house and building survey.

At the conclusion of the Winchester survey in 1979, approximately 2,000 pre-1917 houses and buildings that were still standing had been documented through photographs and data sheets completed in the field. Researchers recorded ownership history, construction dates, architectural style, architect or builder when known, and historic or architectural significance where applicable. The original data sheets are stored in the Henry E. Simonds Memorial Archival Center at 15 High Street; copies are available at the Winchester Public Library.

Susan Keats, Town Archivist at the time, was project coordinator for the survey and directed the research of two Tufts University students and many volunteers. The late Henry E. Simonds, a life-long resident of Winchester who had a vast knowledge of town history, contributed untold hours of tireless work to the survey's completion.

In all, 570 buildings were researched in detail. Of these, approximately 350 houses were documented to be over 100 years old; about 40 had been constructed by the time Winchester was incorporated in 1850. The research also revealed that 14 barns or carriage houses had been converted to residences, and that 75 houses had been moved from their original sites.

As a result of the survey and subsequent applications to the U.S.

Department of the Interior/Heritage Conservation and Recreation Service, the following buildings or neighborhoods have been accepted for listing on the National Register of Historic Places: Josiah Locke House at 195 High Street, Asa Locke Farm at 78 Ridge Street, Sanborn House at 15 High Street, the former Winchester Savings Bank building at 26 Mt. Vernon Street, and the Town Hall at 71 Mt. Vernon Street. In addition, Winchester Center has been accepted as the Winchester Center Historic District.

But because these listings only hint at the architectural riches revealed by the survey, the Winchester Historical Society decided to commemorate Winchester's architectural heritage in a book that residents could use and enjoy. We hope this book will stimulate interest in the architecture of the town and encourage preservation of our noteworthy buildings. They are a reflection of who we are and where we have been— of an era when quality workmanship and good design mattered. They are eloquent reminders of timeless values in a hurried world.

Many people contributed their time and effort to produce this book. Special appreciation is due to Kevin Stevens for conducting research far beyond his role as writer of the text; to Robert M. LaVallee for photographing the houses for the walking tours; to Warburton K. VerPlanck and Virginia M. Sorenson for the walking tour maps; to Andrew Eisenmann, Margaret Harvey, William O'Connor, and Marcia Wood for writing the essays for the walking tours; to Dorothy Wadsworth for fund raising; to Nancy Schrock for the special hand binding of copies for our major donors; to Rose Morrison for typing; and to Susan Keats for consulting on historical matters. Finally, thanks to Jane Robbins who played a pivotal part in the entire development and production of this book.

Ragnhild M. Bairnsfather
Project Coordinator

Overview

Winchester's outstanding Victorian period architecture never fails to impress first-time visitors to the town. Street after street of homes and public buildings combine to create an impression of uniform beauty and architectural integrity. Nestled among hills, ponds, and woods, they exude a comfort and quiet that belie their proximity to a bustling Boston.

Winchester is indeed a rare example of a well-preserved Victorian suburb, but it is more as well. Behind the rich and complex facades of its buildings is an equally rich and complex political, industrial, and cultural heritage. The story of this heritage is the basis for understanding how Winchester came to be the beautiful town it is today, and for appreciating and preserving it.

The seeds for the formation of Winchester were planted in the 1630s, when the original settlers of Charlestown began to explore the wilderness to their west. Over the following three centuries, Winchester went through three clearly defined phases: rural, industrial, and residential. Each phase made a distinctive contribution to the town's architectural development, moving Winchester closer to the way it looks today.

The railroad was central to the social and economic development of the town. In fact, Winchester might not even exist had the builders of the Boston & Lowell Railroad not decided to route their tracks through what was then predominantly rural South Woburn. The railroad served first as a key ingredient to the town's industrial growth; later, when a convenient commuter rail service was added, it helped transform Winchester into an attractive residential suburb by persuading many Boston professionals to build their homes here.

But development of Winchester owed as much to the initiative of its residents as it did to external social and economic forces. Winchester was incorporated by people from abutting sections of Medford, Woburn, and Charlestown whose beliefs and interests set them apart from their "mother" towns. Only through their direct efforts did this separateness become official in the form of a distinct new community, Winchester. After the Civil War, when Winchester began to experience some of the negative fallout of large-scale industrialization, individual townspeople again took initiative, working hard and with remarkable vision to preserve Winchester from the overindustrialized fate of many other New England towns. Today, the arrangement of houses, the layout of the streets, and the attractive parks are a testament to their success.

The pages that follow, therefore, do not relate so much a history of Winchester as of Winchester's people—the people who built its houses and buildings, and how they came to do it. Every house, street, and neighborhood has its own story, and this book relates the most interesting of them.

Part I describes the town as it existed before 1830, a turning point in Winchester's history. That year marked the coming of the railroad and the first stirrings of desire for a separate town identity. Before 1830, Winchester was an agricultural region, and its buildings were primarily farmhouses of a plain and functional style. Most of these were located in the hills above Cambridge Street referred to in this book as Upland Farms, and once known as West Side Hill.

After 1830, as America prospered and cities grew, house styles became more elaborate and ornate, commonly serving as public displays of individual wealth. Part II describes Winchester's development after the coming of the railroad began to bring in sophisticated and moneyed outsiders. A true town center evolved and flourished, and along the major roads radiating from that hub—Church, Main, and Washington Streets—three distinct residential neighborhoods sprang up. Each neighborhood has an express character; each contributes its own qualities to the whole.

Part III offers you an opportunity to see the manifestations of Winchester's political, cultural, and economic history first-hand. It is a set of five walking tours that correspond to the neighborhood structure of the text. In just a few hours' walk, you can experience the architectural heritage of a truly unique Victorian town.

Part I

Laying the Foundations: Winchester Farms and Families, 1638–1830

(Overleaf)
The Edmund and Thaddeus Parker House, probably built shortly after the Revolutionary War and burned down in the 1890s. This photo, one of the oldest owned by the Winchester Historical Society, dates from around 1830. Note the Greek Revival–style doorway that had been added to this otherwise classic Federal style, center-chimney house. The house was located on the southeast corner of Cambridge and Pond Streets.

(Inset) The B. F. Thompson family, c. 1835.

Introduction

Imagine Winchester with only a sprinkling of farms, mills, and rustic houses; with broad expanses of farmland, meadow, and forest; and with only a few dirt roads to connect its scattered residents to the growing towns of Medford and Woburn. A difficult image for us to conjure when we look at the sophisticated, highly developed Winchester of today, yet one reflective of Winchester's first two centuries. In the early 1600s, the area that is now Winchester was primarily rural, with only the seeds of business and industry, and virtually no sense of identity.

The original settlers of Winchester were English Puritans who came up the Mystic Valley from Charlestown in the middle of the seventeenth century. In 1638 the town of Charlestown granted sections of the Winchester valley to over sixty freemen. Most, including Increase Nowell and John Harvard, never lived here, and many sold their allotments to those who decided to settle permanently. These settlers found a region with an abundance of timber for building, good land for farming, water

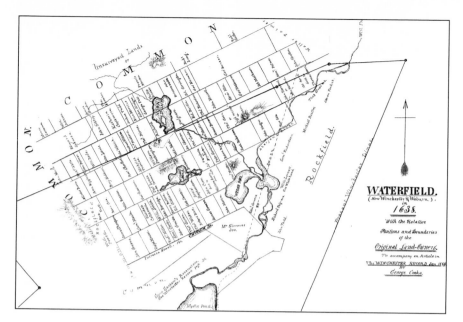

A 1638 map of Waterfield, the name by which part of Winchester was called by early settlers.

power for mills, and a setting that has helped to make Winchester such an attractive place to live ever since.

Five large landowners dominated the early history of the town: the Converses settled the Center; the Richardsons the land north of the Center; the Symmeses the land south of the Center; the Gardners the plains between Upper Mystic Lake and Cambridge Street, and the Johnson/Thompsons the land west of Cambridge Street. Other important families moved in later: the Lockes, the Carters, and the Wymans near the end of the seventeenth century, and the Russells, the Parkers, and the Brooks in the eighteenth century.

These families set the tone for the region. Their men were more than farmers: they were also magistrates, deacons, town officials, and military officers who shaped the town and its character. Often hard-headed, many engaged in suits over property, slander, and right-of-way. But they also did much that was positive, and the town's traditional neighborhood names still proclaim their influence: Symmes Corner, Richardson's Row, Wyman's Plains. For two centuries the names of Winchester's first families weaved through local history, binding places and events, and when the drive to incorporate the town of Winchester was mounted in the 1840s, these families were at its heart.

Laying the Foundations: Winchester Farms and Families, 1638–1830

But progress to this point was slow. Early explorers, inspired by the many lakes and ponds, called the region Waterfield, but the named passed out of use by 1700. Until incorporation in 1850, the land was in fact part of three different towns. Most, including what is now the town center and the whole northern and northwestern section of the town, was part of Woburn. Land south of the Center and east of the Mystic Lakes was in Medford. The remaining section—west of the Mystic Lakes and south of High Street—was part of Charlestown and known as "Charlestown End." This division existed for over two hundred years and affected people's attitudes about the town even after incorporation.

A more important socioeconomic division, however, was between the western and eastern parts of town. The west, including Wyman's Plains, Cambridge Street, and the area west of Cambridge Street called West Side Hill, remained agricultural long after incorporation. It is still the most rural part of town and contains some fine old farmhouses. The eastern section, on the other hand, pursued commercial and industrial development. Though also farmers, its residents established early industries like shoemaking, milling, and tanning. Because water power was necessary for many of these trades, this region developed along the Aberjona River. By the end of the eighteenth century there were three distinct settlements parallel to the river: Richardson's Row, Black Horse Village, and Symmes Corner.

Main roads ran through both sections, serving to separate them even further. The settlements in the east were on or near Main Street, the central artery between Medford and Woburn, which existed from at least 1646. Cambridge Street, formerly Plain Street, was the main thoroughfare on the west side, which early settlers laid in 1643 to provide a route from Cambridge to Woburn. A single road called Driver's Lane that ran along the present course of Church Street connected the east and west sides. The only other roads in town for most of this period were Richardson's Row, now Washington Street; Cross Street in the east; and Ridge Street and High Street in the west. Farms were self-contained and people traveled little.

It would take nearly two centuries and the arrival of the railroad for Winchester to change much. Until the 1830s, it remained a disparate, scattered community with recognizably different sections and only a few dominant families to shape their character.

West Winchester

The architectural heritage of early western Winchester is primarily agricultural. Many buildings that are now residences were once the homesteads and outbuildings of large farms. All buildings remaining from this period are on the three roads laid out in the seventeenth century: Cambridge Street, High Street, and Ridge Street. Those along Cambridge Street usually belonged to farms that stretched east onto Wyman's Plains. Those on High and Ridge were part of Upland Farms, the hilly but fertile region to the west that was settled by two of the most important families in the history of Winchester, the Johnsons and the Lockes.

Captain Edward Johnson was one of the original explorers of the Mystic Valley and a member of the Charlestown church commission that founded the town of Woburn. In addition to farming, he and his descendants participated in town, colony, and state affairs. Captain Johnson was Town Clerk of Woburn, and his son William was a member of the General Court, the highest court in the Massachusetts Bay Colony. Their farmstead covered the area now served by Ridge Street and Johnson Road. Along with the Thompson family, with whom they intermarried, the Johnsons have maintained continuous residence there since Captain Johnson's time. In fact, the oldest house in Winchester, situated at 201 Ridge Street just north of the Vinson-Owen school, is on land originally purchased by Edward Johnson. Built in 1711 by his descendant Josiah Johnson, the house has been owned by the Johnson-Thompson family without interruption ever since.

The house is also one of the few early eighteenth-century homes in the country and is a very important landmark in Winchester because of both its age and its association with a single family. Because of extensive renovations in the mid-1700s, in 1837, and again in 1916, the house bears little resemblance to its eighteenth century appearance. Then it would have been a low structure with a single room, upper loft, and large central chimney typical of the First Period style of architecture, which influenced the design of the Johnson-Thompson house. But the current paired sash windows are probably similar to the original windows, and many of the house's interior features are characteristic of houses built at that time.

The Johnson/Thompson Farm along Ridge Street and (now) Johnson Road in the 1800s. The oldest house in Winchester, it was built in 1711 and has remained in the Johnson/Thompson family ever since.

In the 1800s many of the Johnsons moved closer to the center, but brothers Levi and Ezekial Johnson maintained the farm together until it was partitioned in 1854. When Ezekial married in 1820 he built a house across the road, now 202 Ridge Street. Though completely renovated, the house is important because of its age and its place on the early Johnson farmstead. The historical value of these houses is considerable, especially as the early character of the area disappears. Subdivisions now fill the fields and line the roads, but the presence of these old buildings keeps the region in touch with its past.

The presence of the Locke family in Winchester dates from the seventeenth century, when James Locke bought farmland from James Converse. The Locke family was important throughout New England. Samuel Locke was president of Harvard College in the years prior to the American Revolution, and though he did not live in Winchester, many of his relatives did. James Locke's great-grandsons Asa and Josiah were prominent nineteenth century figures. In the 1850s, when the town was having difficulty balancing its budget, Josiah lent the town $900.00 and Asa contributed to the fund that financed the construction of the Lyceum Hall, a building significant to the social and political development of the town.

The Locke brothers also built some beautiful houses, including those on the Philomen Wright–Asa Locke Farm at 78 Ridge Street, the only surviving farm complex in Winchester and one of the few intact early-nineteenth-century farms in the Boston area. The farm is listed in the National Register of Historic Places.

The first man to farm this land was Philomen Wright, a Winchester native who fought in the American Revolution but later left the United States to become the first white settler of Ottawa, Canada. The Canadian government has honored his contribution to their country with a commemorative plaque on the site of the farm. Wright sold the farm to Asa Locke's father in 1800, and Asa bought it in 1804. He built the present farmhouse in 1828, possibly incorporating parts of Wright's old house. The house remained in the Locke family until 1974, when it was sold to the present owners, who continue to operate the farm.

Though the house has features from a variety of eighteenth- and nineteenth-century architectural styles and a barn and a squash house

The Philomen Wright–Asa Locke Farm at 78 Ridge Street is one of the few intact early-19th-century farm complexes in the Boston area. Still run as a farm, it includes a beautiful Federal house, a barn, a squash house, and a small ice house. The Lockes were an important family throughout Winchester history, with each generation contributing to its social, political, and physical development. Their farm is listed in the National Register of Historic Places.

that were added later, all the buildings are on their original foundations and the complex has considerable historical and architectural integrity. Asa Locke also built the house at 68 High Street in 1857; it too has an interesting mix of features, but lacks the integrity of the Farm.

The dominant American architectural style between 1780 and 1830 was Federal, and the beautiful house at 195 High Street, which Josiah Locke built in 1803, is a good example. Listed in the National Register of Historic Places, the house is in excellent condition and has changed little, though later owners added an east ell in the mid–nineteenth century. The house is also notable for its brick ends: Josiah laid the side facing the town with an expensive technique called *Flemish bond,* but used a cheaper method for the side facing the farmland, a common practice at the time.

But most farmers in this area were more interested in function than style and erected buildings we now call simple or *vernacular*—that is, utilitarian houses with basic features and few frills. The closer a region is to its agricultural roots, the simpler its architecture tends to be, and most of the early buildings on the west side, particularly those along Cambridge Street, are vernacular, reflecting the needs of their original occupants.

The two most important families in the Cambridge Street area were the Gardners and the Wymans. Though most of the land in this area originally belonged to Charlestown's chief magistrate, Increase Nowell, he never lived here, and when he died in 1659 the Gardners bought much of his property.

Old Woburn documents frequently mention the Gardner name. Richard Gardner was one of the town's original settlers and lived near Winter Pond as early as 1651, in a house with cellar bricks that he brought over from England. Richard and his descendants owned a pew in the Woburn meeting house and contributed at least one deacon to the church. As the family's holdings grew, its section of Charlestown End became known as "Gardner's Row." In the 1700s, Richard's descendant Edward Gardner built the most distinguished house on the row, the Gardner-Swan House at 89 Cambridge Street. For a long time the town considered this its oldest house, and though we now know this to be untrue, the house is nevertheless one of the few pre-Revolutionary

buildings in Winchester. A good example of the Second Period, or Georgian, architectural style popular between 1720 and 1780, the house has windows set close to the eaves, a large central chimney, and a steeply pitched roof. For most of the nineteenth century the Swan family owned the house and ran a shoe shop in its west ell. In 1931 the barn and ell were converted to residences, now 2 and 7 Gardner Place, respectively.

Another Gardner house is at 105 Cambridge Street. Though known for a long time as the "1776 House," it was not built until after 1825, the year the sisters Sarah and Patience Gardner bought the site from Benjamin Wyman. The house is a good example of the vernacular Federal style, with tight gables and chimneys to the rear. It has had many owners, including the important town figures Abijah Thompson and Joseph Tyler.

The Gardner family was thin on male heirs and the last of that name to live in Winchester was Samuel Gardner. In 1858 he sold the only remaining part of the original Increase Nowell farm to the famous orator

A turn-of-the-century view of the pre-Revolutionary Gardner-Swan house at 89 Cambridge Street, one of a stretch of Gardner-built houses known as "Gardner's Row." In 1931 the barn and ell (which once housed the Gardner family shoe shop) were converted to residences, now numbers 2 and 7 Gardner Place.

and Winchester developer Edward Everett. But the Wyman family bought most of the Gardner land in the late 1700s, and soon the large, flat area east of Cambridge Street became known as Wyman's Plains.

There were Wymans throughout the district from the seventeenth century. John and Francis Wyman were original settlers of Woburn who became important figures in the history of the town of Burlington. One of their descendants, Hezekiah Wyman, settled on the west side of Winchester. An eccentric man known as the "White Horseman," he was famous for his harrassment of the British during their retreat from Concord in 1775. He owned much of the land east of Cambridge Street and lived on the site of what is now 195 Cambridge. Richard Gardner's original 1660 home had been here, and Hezekiah acquired the land in the eighteenth century. Around 1825, Hezekiah's grandson George Wyman built the house that still stands there. Like most houses on the street, it is vernacular, but is distinguished by an elegant entrance and a finely crafted interior.

George Wyman's brothers, Marshall and William, also lived on Cambridge Street. Marshall built the house at 158, a plain Federal-style house with many later period features. William's house at 145 is vernacular. Both of these houses passed into the ownership of the Locke family in the 1860s.

The Wymans owned and tilled their farmland well into the 1840s, and Wyman's Plains became a residential area relatively late in the town's history. But the three brothers provide a good illustration of how farmers of the time were involved in the community. They all participated in town affairs at the time when a sense of self-identity was just emerging in Winchester. Marshall and George were instrumental in establishing the Wyman School, then on Cambridge Street, and Marshall was also a member of the commission to establish a new Congregational Church; he later became one of the church's first deacons. Much like wealthy businessmen today, the farmers of the mid-1800s looked after their own affairs, but also involved themselves philanthropically and politically in the community. In this way the town came to reflect their vision and interests.

Two families of lesser importance were the Parkers and the Russells. Edmund Parker settled in Winchester in the late 1700s. He was a farmer

1

2

3

4

5

Laying the Foundations: Winchester Farms and Families, 1638–1830

The earliest main thoroughfare, Cambridge Street remained a popular choice for homesites well into the late nineteenth century, with many civically prominent families locating there. Number 195 Cambridge Street is the site of the original 1660 home of Richard Gardner, one of the town's first settlers; the house now standing there (photo 1) was the home of George Wyman, whose family founded the first Wyman School. Parts of Number 117 (photo 2), originally a two-story home on 28 acres, may date back to 1775, and the Thaddeus Parker House (photo 3) was built sometime before 1798. Number 122 Cambridge (photo 4) was built around 1866 by John Ayer, active in the building of Winchester Hospital and the Unitarian Church, and number 130 (photo 5) was built by Loring Emerson, a member of the first Board of Selectmen.

and wheelwright and lived on the southeast corner of Cambridge and Pond Streets in what became known as the "Thaddeus Parker House." The house was named after Edmund's younger son, who lived there until his death in 1889 at the age of 95; the house burned to the ground before the end of the century. Parker's elder son, Edmund Jr., lived on the other side of Pond Street in a house built around 1826 that still stands at 287 Cambridge Street.

The Russell family also moved to Winchester in the late eighteenth century. The Revolutionary War veteran Colonel Bill Russell lived on Cambridge Street for several years, and in 1879 his descendants bought a farm north of High Street established by Luke Reed in 1831. They ran it until 1947, when they sold it to Martha Mahoney, whose family continues the market garden tradition. The houses at 228, 232, and 236 Cambridge Street were part of the farm. The buildings all are vernacular farmhouses, and 236 was originally the rear ell of the Dana Fay House, built across the street in 1823. The main part of that house was moved in 1884 to 37–39 Pond Street.

Luke Reed and Dana Fay were minor nineteenth-century figures who nevertheless were instrumental in creating the early west side. Reed owned a good deal of land and initiated many property transactions. His name continually appears on deeds of the time. Fay was a local builder who constructed many of the old houses on Cambridge Street. He was influential in that part of town, and when the issue of incorporation arose in the 1840s he was the leader of a vocal minority of families from the area who opposed it.

As the farming community developed, the purpose of the farms changed. The aim of the original settlers was self-sufficiency: they provided only for themselves. By the end of the eighteenth century, however, the farmers had become traders, with an expanding urban market just south of them. But the roads of the time were little more than rough dirt paths, and they had difficulty getting their produce to this market. Similarly, as the state's population expanded inland after the American Revolution, Boston merchants and importers had trouble delivering their goods to the growing communities outside the city.

The perfect solution to these problems was the Middlesex Canal. It provided an inexpensive and easy method of transporting produce and raw materials into Boston, and manufactured goods out. Cutting right through the middle of Winchester, the canal was a great boon to the farmers here. It bound the community together and involved its residents in the commerce and industry of the state. Built between 1798 and 1803, the canal was the first of many dramatic changes in the nineteenth century that turned Winchester into an industrial, and then a suburban, town.

The canal was a private enterprise. Many of the most influential men in the country were among its subscribers, including Governor John Hancock, John Adams, and John Quincy Adams. The canal was a great success and the canal company showed a profit until 1836, when, because of competition from the recently completed railroad, the canal became virtually obsolete. Ironically, the canal transported the granite ties used in the construction of the railway. This detail is a good example of a pattern frequently seen in the history of the town. Just as the railway ushered in a new era, it also caused the disappearance of much of what characterized early Winchester. No doubt many viewed the demise of the canal with much the same feeling we now have for the vanishing railways. And yet the canal, though filled in, has left a few legacies. Depressions behind Gardner Place, Fletcher Street, and the houses on the west side of Middlesex Street remind us where the canal once ran, and no. 3 Middlesex Street provides a more tangible memory. Once a boathouse on the canal, it was built about 1790 and moved to its present location on the east side of the street in the 1860s.

East Winchester

The Aberjona River was the most important factor in the shaping of east Winchester. The men who settled here used the river's power to develop the community, further their own interests, and lay the industrial foundation of the region. The three most important families on this side of town—the Converses, the Richardsons, and the Symmeses—were the first to harness the power of the river and construct mills. Though the purpose and ownership of these mills changed over the course of Winchester's history, the influence of these families never wavered.

RULES AND REGULATIONS

RATE OF TOLL

ON THE

MIDDLESEX CANAL......UNTIL FURTHER NOTICE.

APRIL 4, 1808.

Proprietors' Records; Middlesex Canal Association Archives

Rate of Toll poster.

In cutting through the heart of Winchester, the Middlesex Canal, built between 1798 and 1803, became a significant contributor to the development of Winchester as an industrial and ultimately a suburban center.

Laying the Foundations: Winchester Farms and Families, 1638–1830

Edward Converse was the first white person to live in Winchester. An enterprising man who established the first ferry from Charlestown to Boston, Converse built a house on the corner of Main Street and Converse Place in 1640. Almost immediately, he took advantage of the river that ran past his door by damming it to power a grist mill. The dam furnished power for a mill of some kind for almost three hundred years, and created a millpond that continues to enhance the beauty of the town center today.

Converse's farm included all of the Center. The site of the Town Hall was his sheep pasture, and the common his cornfield. The mill and farm were successful, and his will revealed him to be a relatively wealthy man. His descendants continued to figure prominently in town affairs, especially his grandson, Captain James Converse, who was famous throughout Massachusetts for his defense of a garrison in Wells, Maine, against the Indian attack of 1692. But ultimately the prominence of the Converses in the Center was eclipsed by the family that did most to develop early industry, the Richardsons.

Three Richardson brothers—Ezekial, Samuel, and Thomas—served on the Charlestown church commission that set up the new town of Woburn. By 1642 they had settled the northeastern part of Winchester, establishing farms connected by what is now Washington Street, then called Richardson's Row. The road was one of the earliest in the town and soon became the center of a busy settlement as the family expanded. All three of the brothers raised large families, and their descendants touched every part of Winchester's history.

Toward the end of the seventeenth century the Richardsons built the town's first sawmill near Forest Street. The mill, which provided lumber for many of the settlement's early houses, was powered by Saw-mill Brook, a stream that ran from a marshy meadow now covered by the North Reservoir, and that disappeared when the reservoir was built. In the late eighteenth century Abel Richardson bought the Converse mill, and Joseph and Thomas Richardson built a large gristmill on Horn Pond Brook. In this way the family came to control the town's only industries.

The mills were important not only because they contributed to the development of the town, but also because they provided ideal locations for later industries. In 1840 John Cutter took over and improved the Horn Pond Brook mill, and his descendants transformed it from a grist-mill to one that performed many industrial tasks. The Converse mill had many incarnations even before the 1830s, when Samuel Steele Richardson built a complex of shops in and around it. He sold it to Harrison Parker, who used it to cut mahogany and rosewood. Parker sold it to Joel Whitney, who established the Whitney Machine Company that ran on the same site until 1911, completing over 250 years of industrial continuity. This changing hands illustrates well how pre-industrial, agricultural Winchester made its transition to the industrial nineteenth century.

An offshoot of the mills were the stores and shops that sprang up along Richardson's Row. By the end of the eighteenth century the area had blacksmiths, wheelwrights, saddlers, coopers, joiners, and men engaged in various leather-related trades. The Richardson name figured in every trade, and it is safe to say that the family dominated business at the time. They were especially prominent in shoemaking, the most important small industry of early Winchester.

We have already noted that part of the Gardner-Swan House at 89 Cambridge Street was originally a shoe shop. Many families participated in this popular cottage industry, making shoes either in their house or, as in the Swans's case, in a little shop at the side of the house. The practice was so widespread that many families paid their taxes with shoes, and the town of Woburn sometimes even paid its colony taxes in the same way. By the end of the eighteenth century, home shoe manufacturing was a thriving industry, though one usually practiced only in winter when farming was not possible. It was customary to work from dawn until ten at night, October to April, at the slow and laborious tasks of cutting leather, shaping soles, fitting the pieces, and stitching the whole shoe together by hand. By the 1830s, in a village of only seventy houses, there were thirty-five shoe shops in operation, and the Richardsons owned at least twelve of them. Winchester's shops were in fact part of a large industry throughout northern Massachusetts that fed off the leather and tanning industries established in the early eighteenth century. Woburn was always a "leather town" and a supplier of raw materials for the Winchester shops.

Laying the Foundations: Winchester Farms and Families, 1638–1830

We can get a good idea of what the shoe shops looked like externally by examining the vernacular house at 146 Forest Street. The small size of the building (10 × 13) and its closeness to the road (ten feet) suggest that it was originally a shoe shop. Part of the present building may have been an earlier shoe shop owned by the twins Caleb and Joshua Richardson in the late 1700s. Caleb lived in a vernacular house still standing at 465–467 Washington Street, which he built before 1831. Caleb and Joshua also farmed and ran the gristmill on Horn Pond Brook before they sold it to John Cutter.

The house that now stands at 597 Washington Street was another Richardson shoe shop. Zachariah Richardson moved the old building, perhaps built as early as 1794, from its former location farther south on Richardson's Row when he set up his business in 1818. The shop was actually in the front yard of his residence, the Zachariah Richardson House, which still stands at 7 Sunset Road. Another Richardson house is at 569 Washington. All these buildings are on property originally granted to Samuel Richardson in 1641. None is architectually noteworthy, though 7 Sunset is a curious jumble of eighteenth and nineteenth century styles.

The Richardsons gave the town many selectmen, soldiers, and deacons. They also helped to preserve the town's heritage. In 1831, in accordance with a requirement of the legislature that each town furnish material for the construction of a state map, Bartholomew Richardson surveyed the town. When the *Winchester Record* published the map in 1886, the amateur historian Nathaniel A. Richardson helped designate the homesteads. This map provides valuable evidence for the dating of early buildings, and it is fitting that the Richardson family contributed to it.

In 1724 William Richardson bought over thirty acres of land along Main Street, south of Richardson's Row, from Robert Converse and James Richardson. Some time between then and 1728 he built the biggest house in Winchester at the time, a two-story, forty-foot square building he called his "mansion home," at the corner of Main Street and Black Horse Terrace. He was evidently very proud of it, but in 1728 he sold it to a Captain Isaac Dupee, who gradually turned the mansion into a lodging house of sorts. By 1743, when David Wyman bought the building, it was known as the Black Horse Tavern, one of the most important landmarks in the history of early Winchester. For the next century it served as a center for town life and attained a reputation throughout Massachusetts as one of the best rural taverns. During colonial times it was one of the only meeting places for the farmers of southern Woburn and northern Medford and a favorite stopping place for travelers to and from Boston, particularly farmers bringing produce to market. During the Revolutionary War, military companies were assembled or dismissed at the tavern. When stage routes were set in New England in the late eighteenth century, the tavern benefited from the business as Winchester was a likely first stop on the main route between Boston and Portsmouth.

Public meetings, dances, singing schools, and neighborhood gatherings took place at the Black Horse Tavern. A natural focal point, the tavern soon became the center of the second east side settlement, Black Horse Village. In the 1770s David Wyman's brother Paul established the first store in Winchester at the junction of Main and Washington Streets, and by the early nineteenth century a blacksmith's shop, wheelwright's shop, and a number of residences also clustered around the tavern. In the 1830s engineers and construction workers for the new railroad arrived and provided the tavern with a brisk business; ironically, however, the railroad also led to the tavern's downfall by making the stage routes obsolete and depriving the inn of its most reliable custom. After the 1830s, the tavern business dwindled but the village continued to thrive, especially as a residential neighborhood for prominent local men. In this way Black Horse Village was pivotal in the transition of Winchester from a farming community into a residential suburb.

In 1892, businessman and real estate speculator Preston Pond tore down the tavern. A shoe shop that was next to it became the back ell of the house at 403 Main Street, but otherwise the only part of the Black Horse Tavern still in existence is the barn, which was moved to the rear of 8 Oak Street when the tavern was pulled down.

Black Horse Village was near the southernmost point of Woburn. Beyond it was Medford and the 300 acres that the town of Charlestown granted to Zachariah Symmes in 1636. Symmes's land comprised almost all of Winchester south of Black Horse Village and east of the old In-

Originally built between 1724 and 1728 by William Richardson as his "mansion home," this large house at the corner of Main Street and Black Horse Terrace was then sold and turned into a lodging house. For over a century, the Black Horse Tavern served as meeting place and entertainment center for travelers and townspeople alike. The famous landmark was torn down by Preston Pond in 1892.

Laying the Foundations: Winchester Farms and Families, 1638–1830

crease Nowell farm along Cambridge Street. Zachariah was the minister of Charlestown Church, and the size of his allotment, the largest given, was evidence of his esteem.

Zachariah farmed the land but did not live on it. His son William built the first Symmes house there along the Aberjona River, on land now part of Manchester Field. In the 1700s the family built two mills and several houses on the river, and a number of old maps even refer to the Aberjona at that point as the Symmes River. At this time the river was part of a tidal estuary and flowed through a salt meadow now flooded by the Upper Mystic Lake. The river entered the lake as far south as the "narrows," near the house that is now the Winchester Boat Club. The Symmes fished the river and lake for bass, perch and alewives, and cut hay on the meadow. Their farm was one of the largest in Winchester, with a broad sheep pasture across from what is now the Rangeley development. The enterprising family also initiated several small industries, including a forge at one of their mills that used local bog iron and produced a rotary engine for an experimental Middlesex Canal steamboat.

In 1715 the Symmeses sold their land east of Main Street to Ebenezer Brooks, and in 1825 Robert Bacon bought their land west of the river. By the end of the eighteenth century they had sold their mill privileges and moved to the part of town most firmly associated with the family today, Symmes Corner.

Captain John Symmes was the first of the family to live at Symmes Corner, building a house at the junction of Grove and Main Street in the 1790s. By then the Symmes family was probably the largest in Winchester. Captain John was a distinguished Revolutionary War veteran, and when he returned from the war he established blacksmith and wheelwright businesses close to his farm. His sons, Deacon John Symmes and Marshall Symmes, both built houses at Symmes Corner that today are among the most beautiful in town. Both houses are excellent examples of the Federal style, and Marshall's house at 230 Main Street is one of the largest Federal period houses in Winchester. It is noteworthy for its pilastered cornerboards, four chimneys, and brick ends, and has remained in the Symmes family since it was built in 1817. Marshall himself lived in the house until his death in 1877.

Deacon John built his house at 212 Main Street in 1807. He and his son Luther continued the wheelwright business established by Captain John while Marshall ran the blacksmith shop. These shops were an important part of Winchester's early industry, providing, among other things, carts and wagons for the army. In 1804 the town's two most prolific families were united when Deacon John married Pamela Richardson, who afterward ran the first formal school in Winchester out of their home. John was a deacon of the First Congregational Church from 1818 until his death in 1860 and held many important offices in the town of Medford. When Winchester was incorporated in 1850, both John and Marshall signed a petition with other residents of Medford asking not to be included in the new town. When Winchester later chose John as selectman he refused to serve, though Marshall did serve as assessor.

John's son Luther became an important town figure. He made up for his father's reluctance to participate in town affairs by serving as selectman, cemetery commissioner, and board member of the Mystic Water Works. He was also a founding member of the Winchester Historical Society and wrote a great deal on town history for the *Winchester Record* and the *Winchester Star*. It is appropriate that a scion of the Symmeses and the Richardsons, families with such deep roots in the town, should do so much to preserve the town's heritage. It is also fitting that the houses that Luther's father and uncle built are among the town's finest examples of early architecture.

The Symmeses round out our picture of early Winchester, which by 1830 was on the verge of significant changes. The arrival of the railroad in the 1830s began a process of change in Winchester from a farming community into an industrial and residential suburb, and saw the decline of early town landmarks like the Middlesex Canal and the Black Horse Tavern. Yet in spite of these changes, the town has a continuous history bound by tradition, architecture, and, most important, people. No matter what the era, the town has always had a sense of the past and of its own integrity, a sense that has passed from generation to generation. The same family names fill the history of Winchester beyond 1830 and provide a link between the early and modern town.

Symmes Corner, at the intersection of Main, Grove, and Bacon Streets, took its name from the Symmes family properties that surrounded it. Pictured here are old photos of two of the three Symmes homes that still stand there, and one non-Symmes home that also faced the square: the Deacon John Symmes House (photo 1); the 1721 Brooks-LeBosquet House (photo 2); and the 1817 Marshall Symmes House (photo 3), still occupied by Symmes descendants. The first two houses were part of Medford before Winchester's incorporation.

1

2

3

Part II

Emergence of a True Victorian Town: Winchester Neighborhoods, 1830–1916

(Overleaf)
Trolley #1014 to Boston, one of 85 trains
and trolleys that ran between Boston and
Winchester daily and that helped make Winchester an "ideal" place to live. This photo
was taken around 1910; today there are only
11 trains to and from Boston each day. This
is progress?

(Inset) Shop at corner of Main opposite
Railroad (Mt. Vernon).

Chapter 1

Winchester Center: Commercial, Religious, and Political Hub

The history of Winchester Center begins in the 1830s, when the forces that led to incorporation first appeared. The most important of these forces was the Boston and Lowell Railroad, which solidified the increasing self-subsistence of the South Woburn area. In the 1830s and 1840s, stores, shops, and small industries flourished around the new railroad line and the station on Main Street, providing local residents with a much more convenient source of goods and services than the distant village centers of Medford and Woburn.

Ultimately, the railroad also expanded the commercial center by creating a commuter population. From the 1830s on, Winchester was a popular place of residence for Boston businessmen and professionals, a quiet haven away from the bustling city. Many of these new residents eventually transferred their businesses and practices to Winchester itself.

With its commercial center well established, the town's homogeneous, Christian population of nearly 1,000 residents soon desired its own church. Distance from the Woburn Church and a growing sense of self-identity led to the establishment in 1840 of the Congregational Church of South Woburn on the slope between Church Street and Wedge Pond. The presence of an independent place of worship in the Center gave the community a cultural and social cohesion that paralleled the town's commercial and industrial growth.

But though South Woburn had developed its own identity, it still lay within the three different towns whose borders were established in the seventeenth century: Desiring a unity of government and development of its own, the villagers began a movement toward the inevitable: incorporation as an independent municipality.

Political differences between South Woburn and its parent town of Woburn heightened this desire. South Woburn was predominantly Whig, Woburn mostly Democratic. During the 1840s, South Woburn voters increasingly felt that Woburn municipal government did not represent their best interests. Clashes over the use of Andrew Jackson's Surplus Fund and the appropriation of Woburn town money for the creation of a South Woburn street generated enough bad feeling to get South Woburn residents talking seriously about incorporation. When the Massachusetts Whig Party came to power in 1848, the leaders of South Woburn saw an opportunity to push plans for a new town forward. Many of the movement's leaders, including F. O. Prince, mayor of Boston between 1877 and 1881, were talented newcomers to the town with no sentimental attachment to Woburn or Medford. They worked behind the scenes, circulating a petition for presentation to the legislature's Committee on Towns in February 1850. In spite of opposition by the town of Woburn; the west side faction led by Dana Fay; and many of the old families, including the Johnsons and the Symmeses; the bill of incorporation passed easily in both the House and the Senate. The town of Winchester was officially born.

The name "Winchester" was chosen while the petition for incorporation was being prepared. A committee was formed to come up with something suitable: Mystic, Wyoming, Columbus, Harmony, and Appleton were some of the suggestions, but none had any strong relevancy. Then F. O. Prince told the naming committee that if the town were named Winchester, a wealthy Boston merchant living in Watertown, Col. William P. Winchester, would more than likely present the town

In the 1830s and 1840s, a new center of commerce developed around the railroad line that cut through Main Street. Formation of a new church to serve the people in the area helped solidify the members' growing sense of identity as a separate community, and gave the final impetus for Winchester's incorporation in 1850.

with a large sum of money. Indeed, he gave $3,000 to go towards the building of a town hall, a large sum of money at the time. But thirty-eight years later the gift was only enough to finance the building of the Town Hall clock tower.

In the fifty years between incorporation and the turn of the century, Winchester Center changed dramatically. Commercially, the town center passed from an early industrial area into the business hub of a prosperous residential community, with industry moved out to the north end of town. Socially, Winchester changed from a quiet mid-nineteenth-century village into a thriving town with all the social and civic features of a successful twentieth-century American municipality. Together, these changes molded Winchester Center as it is today.

Business and Industry

Geography and chance brought the railroad to Winchester. In 1830, partly at the urging of Daniel Webster, the Massachusetts General Court granted a charter allowing a group of cotton industrialists in Lowell to begin construction of the Boston and Lowell Railroad. The cotton merchants were looking for a cheap way to transport large quantities of raw cotton from Boston up to Lowell, and manufactured cloth back. Road transportation was too expensive, and the Middlesex Canal was frozen for four months of the year. One of the industrialists, Patrick Johnson, had heard about the development of the steam locomotive in England, where the first public railway in the world had opened in 1825. He persuaded his colleagues to help him finance a railroad between Boston and Lowell.

The investors chose a route suited to freight transportation: straight up the natural corridor of the Mystic Valley. They did not plan a passenger service and laid track in as direct a line as possible while avoiding the busy villages of Woburn, Wilmington, and Medford. When they had finished, however, the planners saw that carrying passengers would be an excellent source of revenue and they built a number of stations along the way, including South Woburn Station on Main Street. In this way Winchester, scarcely a village at the time, fortuitously received just the impetus it needed to grow into a thriving town.

Even before it was completed, the railroad was generating business. The engineers and construction crews, who arrived in the early 1830s to survey the land and lay track, gave the Black Horse Tavern and local stores a roaring trade. Some local industries also profited, particularly the blacksmith and ironworking shop of Francis and Nathan Johnson. They furnished a good deal of ironmongery for the new railway and monopolized the construction of tie bolts.

People came from all over to observe the construction. In 1830, when there were only 23 miles of railway in the entire United States, the Boston and Lowell was a technological novelty. The scattered farm dwellers of South Woburn had the opportunity to witness something that very few people in the world had seen. When the first passenger train passed through Winchester on May 27, 1835, thousands of observers lined the tracks. No doubt many of these observers became regular customers of the railroad themselves; South Woburn Station opened in 1837, and rail service to the town has been continuous ever since.

The railroad stimulated the growth of business and industry in the Center in three ways: it provided an accessible, efficient means of transporting goods and materials; it generated a steady flow of traffic, creating a market for local shopkeepers; and it formed a natural center where townspeople congregated and fraternized. This growth occurred at a critical point in the development of industry in Massachusetts. The 1830s was a decade of great change. The rise of the factory system; the substitution of immigrant for native labor; the improvement of machinery; and the harnessing of water power turned Massachusetts into a strong industrial state with great centers at Lowell, Lawrence, and Fall River.

In its own small way, Winchester participated in this development. Several inventive and entrepreneurial businessmen from the surrounding area recognized the advantages that the railroad presented in South Woburn and moved in quickly. Between 1835 and 1845, four men in particular transformed the town center into a small industrial hub: Samuel Steele Richardson, Benjamin Thompson, Harrison Parker, and Joel Whitney. These men had a number of things in common. They all came from outside the immediate area; they had ideas and were prepared to take risks; and they were all associated in some way with the old Converse mill, the industrial center of the town for over 250 years.

It is stated, on good authority, that on and after the first of June, tickets to and from this town will be sold in packages of six for a dollar, the season tickets to be $68 per year, being an increase of $4 per quarter. This enormous increase in season tickets is the most suicidal policy which the Directors of the Corporation can possibly adopt. The result will inevitably be, that persons having an idea of removing into this vicinity will abandon the idea and locate in or nearer the city, where the expense of travel will not be so great, and many of those now owning real estate in these parts will not hesitate to sell it at the first opportunity. This will be the practical workings of the short sighted policy of those representing the corporation managing our railroads.

21 May 1864
Middlesex Journal

When track was first laid between Boston and Lowell to carry freight, Winchester just happened to be located along the shortest route. A decision to carry passengers was made shortly thereafter, catapulting Winchester, only a quiet village at the time, into something of a small commercial and industrial hub. When the first passenger train stopped at South Woburn (Winchester Center) station on May 27, 1835, thousands lined the tracks to witness the then-rare spectacle. The beautiful Gothic structure in the photo above is the Lyceum building (corner of Main and Mt. Vernon Streets) in its original glory.

Samuel Steele Richardson, who was related to the many Richardsons on Washington Street, ran a successful shoemaking business in Woburn. Seeing the potential of the new center, he established another shoe shop across the street from the new South Woburn Station. But his biggest move was to purchase the decaying Converse mill and develop it into a complex of shops and small industries. He turned out door knobs and bedsteads on a wood lathe, renting out remaining rooms to two sash and blind businesses, a dye shop, and various manufacturers of shoemaking equipment. The technology of shoe manufacturing was blossoming in the 1830s, and some of the men who rented space from Richardson were at the forefront of their trade. One of them was Amos Whittemore, inventor of a shoe-pegging machine that revolutionized the industry.

1

2

The burgeoning center and railroad attracted outside entrepreneurs to Winchester. Among them were Joel Whitney, who with his son Authur founded and ran the Whitney Machine Shop at Main and Walnut (Mystic Valley Parkway) Streets (the view of Whitney Mill Pond in photo 1 also shows another view of the old Lyceum building after removal of the roof during its first "renovation").

Other industrial entrepreneurs of the era were Samuel Steele Richardson, Benjamin Thompson, and Harrison Parker. Thompson located his tannery on the site of what is now Manchester Field (photo 2); it later became the Waldmeyer Tannery (photo 3). Today, it is hard to imagine Manchester Field as the location of this and other "unsightly" industrial businesses such as Henry Emerson's freight yard (photo 4).

Emergence of a True Victorian Town: Winchester Neighborhoods, 1830–1916

3

4

Another Richardson tenant was Benjamin Thompson, who opened a currier shop in the mill in 1838. An important link in the local shoe-making business, Thompson purchased rough leather from tanners in New Hampshire and Vermont, split it into various thicknesses, finished it, and then sold it in small quantities to the shoemakers scattered throughout the district. Of all the small industries in the Richardson mill, his was the most successful, and in 1844 he built a small shop on the site of what is now Manchester Field. Business continued to thrive, and in 1853 he fulfilled a life-long dream and kept pace with the expanding market by building the Thompson tannery next to his new currier shop. The tannery was the first large-scale factory in Winchester, and materials for its construction came from all over: stone from the quarries of Somerville, lime and cement from Charlestown, and brick and lumber from Medford.

In 1841, Samuel S. Richardson, who had suffered financial difficulties in the 1837 depression, sold the old Converse mill to Harrison Parker, who had married into the Richardson family. Parker moved his mahogany veneer-cutting business there from the Jeduthan Richardson mill near Cross Street, and perfected a new cutting machine that revolutionized the process and ensured his success. For years, teams of eight and ten horses drawing mahogany and rosewood from Boston ships to the Parker mill were a common sight on Winchester streets.

In 1845, Joel Whitney came from Wakefield to Winchester to operate a machine shop and manufacture leather-working machinery in Parker's mill. Like many of the early industrialists, Whitney was an inventor. His patents for veneering machines, printing presses, and a number of machines for splitting and working leather kept him at the leading edge of industrial technology. In 1857, when Parker moved his business to Charlestown to be close to the harbor, the successful Whitney became sole owner of the mill. The Whitney family was the last to run the old Converse mill; Joel's descendants ran the business at that site until 1909, when the town forced them to move north to make way for park development.

By 1855, Winchester Center had a solid industrial base, with expanding concerns in tanning, woodworking, and machine making. North and south of the Center along the Aberjona River, other old mills were revitalized, and Winchester was well on its way to becoming a typical late nineteenth-century industrial New England town. The industries attracted workers, and as the population grew, local business and the commercial center expanded as well. An 1854 map of the town, the first made after incorporation, shows a heavy concentration of small businesses at the center, including grocery and provision stores, livery stables, blacksmith and wheelwright shops, druggists and shoe stores. There has been a post office in the Center since 1841 and a practicing physician's office since 1846. James Bayley built a coal yard next to the Thompson tannery in 1852 and delivered coal to local residents with a horse and cart. Edmund Sanderson and Alvin Taylor ran a well-stocked general store that also served as a meeting place for town citizens. Business had combined with industry and the railroad to create a substantial town with a well-defined center.

Industry continued to grow, and after the Civil War Winchester came into her own as a tanning town. By 1855 Winchester produced over $2 million worth of leather, fourth in the state behind Woburn, Salem, and Peabody. But the years following the war also saw the appearance of forces that ultimately led to the decline of industry and the rise of Winchester as a residential and business community.

There was a change of mood in the town in the 1860s. Since incorporation, the town had continued to attract prosperous citizens who ran businesses in Boston. Though they didn't eclipse the old families, these new arrivals did form a pool of educated, experienced professionals from which the town chose many leaders, selectmen, and legislators. Over the years, men like F. O. Prince, David Skillings, and Forrest Manchester joined with the descendants of the Richardsons and Johnsons and others to create and mold the town into a retreat from the hectic pace of city life—a quiet suburb reflecting the status of its residents. Industry never fully disappeared from Winchester, but gradually the town managed to move it all to the north end of town, leaving the Center free for the development of parks, residences, and nonindustrial businesses.

One of the first public demonstrations of this change of mood occurred in 1865, when Andrew Shepard proposed building a large tannery next to the one already standing on our present Manchester Field.

The town responded so negatively to his proposal that Shepard did not exercise his option to build. In the 1870s the town openly discussed its protective feelings and in 1882 formed the Village Improvement Association (VIA). Though regarded by some critics as ineffectual, the VIA did beautify the Center considerably by planting trees and shrubs, building fountains and concrete walks, and improving the town common and other plots of greenery. Though it only lasted fifteen years, the VIA created an important function that the Park Commission and Planning Board took over and continues to fill today.

The movement to beautify Winchester reached its zenith in the 1890s, when the Metropolitan District Commission built its parkway system and a group of residents saw an opportunity to rid the center of the unsightly cluster of industries on and near Manchester Field, including the tannery and the coal yard, a lumber yard, a railway freight yard, and a line of tenements. Forrest Manchester and Edwin Ginn led the fight to tear down these eyesores and, with the MDC, transform the area into a park and playground parallel to the Mystic Valley Parkway. Though there was some opposition, Manchester and Ginn's group convinced the railroad to move its freight yard north of the center. The owners of the lumber and coal yards, Alexis Cutting and Henry Emerson, agreed to move out on Main Street, near Skillings Road. The Waldmyers, who had bought the tannery from the Thompson family in 1870, were making only a marginal profit and were willing to sell. In this way the town created Manchester Field, named after Forrest Manchester, in 1895. By 1900 the only industry left in the center was the Whitney Machine Company, and that also moved north to Main Street in 1911.

The commercial development of the Center, on the other hand, did not slacken, but kept pace with the growth of the population, which had doubled to 2,646 between the year of incorporation and 1870. During the last quarter of the nineteenth century, Winchester Center acquired many of the large commercial buildings that gave it the architectural character it has today. Three that appeared in the 1870s and 1880s were particularly important: the Brown and Stanton Block, the White Building, and the White Block.

In 1879, at the corner of Main and Mt. Vernon Streets, George P. Brown and Jacob H. Stanton, Jr., built the handsome Queen Anne style

—THE—
ANNUAL RECEPTION AND DINNER
—OF THE—
❖ WINCHESTER ❖
VILLAGE IMPROVEMENT ASSOCIATION
WILL BE HELD IN THE
—TOWN ∴ HALL,—
THURSDAY EVENING, MARCH 6TH, 1890.

His Excellency, Gov. Brackett, Hon. F. O. Prince, Hon. Henry B. Metcalf of Pawtucket, R. I., General J. M. Corse, Mr. R. C. Metcalf, Mr. C. O. Billings, and others, will be guests of the Association.

MRS. A. E. COFFIN, SOLOIST.

MISS MARION H. WHITTAKER, OF BOSTON, WHISTLER.

Reception at 5.30 and Dinner at 6.30 sharp.

Tickets, $1.00, to be obtained at Dr. Brown's or of the Committee.

It is hoped that an early application will be made for tickets so that the Committee can make preparations to accommodate all. The following-named gentlemen and ladies have been named as a

RECEPTION COMMITTEE:

Mr. and Mrs. A. E. Whitney,	Mr. and Mrs. J. F. Dorsey,
" " " J. W. Suter,	" " " H. A. Emerson,
" " " T. S. Spurr,	" " " S. J. Elder,
" " " H. L. Barnard,	" " " B. T. Church,
" " " C. F. Lunt,	" " " E. A. Smith,
" " " Preston Pond,	" " " S. W. McCall,
" " " F. H. Manchester,	" " " W. F. Fitch,
Mr. Geo. G. Stratton.	

S. W. TWOMBLY, ⎫ Committee
S. W. REYNOLDS, ⎬ of
S. C. SMALL, ⎭ Arrangements.

- - Star Print, Miller's Block. - -

Fortunately for today's residents, a group of citizens who had chosen to live in Winchester precisely to escape the noise and grime of commerce gradually engineered the removal of Winchester industry out of the Center. And in 1882, the Village Improvement Society was formed to beautify the Center with plantings and parks. As you can see in the idyllic photo at right, by the turn of the century Manchester Field had been restored to a pastoral park for the townspeoples' pleasure.

Annual Banquet,
WINCHESTER VILLAGE IMPROVEMENT ASSOCIATION,
TOWN HALL, - - March 6, 1890.

MENU

OYSTERS.
Escalloped and Raw

ENTREES.
Chicken Croquettes with French Peas
Cream Fritters with Wine Sauce
Chicken Patties, Potato Croquettes

COLD MEATS.
Roast Turkey   Chicken

SALADS.
Lobster

SWEETS.
Macedoine of Fruit in Jelly
Charlotte Russe
Frozen Pudding

SHERBETS
Lemon   Orange   Raspberry Harlequin

ICE CREAM.
Vanilla   Strawberry   Chocolate Harlequin

CAKE.
Almond   Citron   Currant   Chocolate
Lady Fingers   Macaroons   Cocoanuts   Fancy Decorated

FRUIT.
Bananas   Grapes   Oranges

Tea   Coffee

J. TYLER HICKS & CO., Caterers, - - - BOSTON.

ANNUAL RECEPTION AND DINNER
—— OF THE ——
Winchester ✳ Village ✳ Improvement ✳ Association,
TOWN HALL,
Thursday Evening, March 6th, 1890.

RECEPTION AT 5.30. . . . . . . , DINNER 6.30.

Tickets, $1.00 Each.

block named after them. Brown was the town druggist, Town Clerk, and Postmaster, and a founder of the Winchester Unitarian Society. Stanton was a prosperous grocer who had "two teams constantly delivering." Both men moved their businesses to the new block as soon as it was completed, and the building became an important business center. But in the early years the block was not confined to commerce; it also contained the post office, public library, and the town's municipal offices. Harmony Hall, located on the second floor of the building, was the site of many social events and, in 1882, the first public Episcopal service in Winchester. Though later owners put a new facade on the first floor in the 1950s, the block still presides grandly over the town center, and the second floor presents some beautiful features of the Queen Anne style: decorative panel brickwork, gables with vergeboard trim and round-headed windows, and a distinctive corner tower with a conical roof.

Next door to the Brown and Stanton Block, at 5–13 Mt. Vernon Street, is the White Block. Samuel B. White, who owned a good deal of real estate in Winchester Center, put up this building, and the White Building at 568–572 Main Street around 1890. Though neither is as architecturally distinctive as the Brown and Stanton building, both were part of the growing commercial landscape of commercial Winchester and

In the late Victorian era, Winchester acquired many of its outstanding commercial buildings. These views of the Center, all taken between 1890 and 1922, show a bustling shopping area not significantly different from the way it looks today.

Emergence of a True Victorian Town: Winchester Neighborhoods, 1830–1916

Winchester Center: Commercial, Religious, and Political Hub

37

Savings Bank, Winchester, Mass.

provided many storekeepers and professionals with good central locations from which to do business.

Banking arrived in Winchester in 1871 when a group of businessmen incorporated the Winchester Savings Bank. The bank occupied a single room in an old house by the grade crossing until 1880 when it moved to the Brown and Stanton Block. In 1892 the architects Edwin

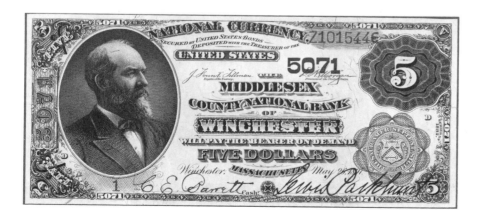

Emergence of a True Victorian Town: Winchester Neighborhoods, 1830–1916

K. and William E. Blaikie designed the impressive Richardson Romanesque building at 26 Mt. Vernon Street, home of the bank until late 1979. Listed in the National Register of Historic Places, the building has a beautiful brick and sandstone exterior and a Queen Anne corner tower very like the one atop the nearby Brown and Stanton Block. Though the interior was completely remodeled in 1965, the exterior is exactly as it was when it was built. Perhaps it is appropriate that this building, symbol of Winchester's arrival as a commercial Victorian town, is one of the finest commercial structures in the center.

Social and Civic Development

Just as the railroad provided an impetus for the town's economic growth, the church gave the townspeople a central meeting place that helped create a sense of community, especially during the two decades framing incorporation, the 1840s and 1850s. But while the railroad arrived from outside the community and created the Center almost by chance, the church came from within, the result of careful planning by the residents themselves. The railroad was an economic force that required the town to adapt to it; the church was an expression of the needs and will of the people.

Until 1840 the residents of South Woburn had worshiped at the Woburn Congregational Church. But as the new Center emerged, the townspeople set about establishing the institutions that would give the area social and legal independence. They began in 1839 by petitioning the General Court for their own church, with many now-familiar citizens leading the crusade: Zachariah Symmes, Marshall Wyman, Sumner Richardson, and Benjamin Thompson. They argued that the Woburn Church was too distant for many on the south side of town, particularly the infirm, and that a ministry in South Woburn would widen the sphere of the church's influence. These valid reasons belied a deeper motive— to obtain more freedom for South Woburn in the management of its own affairs. The Woburn Church, reluctant to part with a sizable portion of its membership postponed discussion of the petition and then dismissed it altogether. Not to be denied, the people of South Woburn ignored this dismissal and formed their own Congregational Society in May of 1840. Four days after its formation, the society bought land for a new church from Thomas Collins and the Boston and Lowell Railroad. Gardner Symmes built the new church, a simple white meetinghouse with belfry and steeple flanked by two rows of horse sheds. Once established, the new church courteously requested written dismissal from its parent, and the Woburn church had no choice but to grant it to the men and women of South Woburn.

When the church burned to the ground in 1853, the Congregational Society immediately began work on a new church on the same site. Judging from the attention given its progress by the Woburn Journal and the Middlesex Journal, construction of the new church generated considerable interest. Though there was some controversy over the cross placed atop the spire, the people of the town generally thought that the Romanesque building was stately and beautiful enough for its high purpose, and they enjoyed having a larger and more elaborate place of worship than the old meetinghouse. The Society remodeled the building in 1884, and in 1926 rebuilt the western end; added a chancel, a new organ, and a marble communion table; and built a parish house in the rear. The church remains today what its original builders hoped it would be: one of the most distinguished buildings in the town.

In mid-nineteenth-century America the church was more than a place of worship; it was the center of town life, the place where people met and talked. Most social life was church-related, with many church-organized picnics, lectures, and concerts. Church news and sermons were often published in the papers and correspondents often expressed religious views that today would be considered inappropriate in a newspaper. But in those days the church was part of the fabric of daily life.

Though the church was the most important social and cultural center in Winchester, other organizations provided an opportunity, particularly for young people, to meet, talk, and learn. The 1840s and 1850s were the heyday of lyceums and literary associations—groups that formed for, among other things, the "social and literary improvement upon the part of the young of both sexes." These groups met in private homes or local halls to read original compositions, discuss the issues of the day, and in general to cultivate social faculties. Their members often invited

Interior of the newly rebuilt Congregational Church in 1890.

prominent professional lecturers to address them, and up to the beginning of the Civil War the lyceum lecture was a popular feature of almost every New England town.

For lack of an adequate meeting place, the South Woburn Social Lyceum, formed in 1846, did not last long. But in 1851 local residents, including Asa Locke and H. K. Stanton, put up money for the construction of Lyceum Hall, which Sumner Richardson built on the northeast corner of Main and Mt. Vernon Streets. The present structure bears little resemblance to the Gothic Revival, four-story original that, with its distinctive facade, dominated the town center in the 1800s. The Lyceum contained store and office space and a hall that sat 450 people. Until the town built the Lyceum, it had only the vestry of the Congregational Church in which to meet, so the new building must have seemed magnificent to the newly incorporated town. The Lyceum was the site of town meetings for thirty-five years, and remained the most important civic building until the construction of the Town Hall in 1887. Dances, entertainments, singing schools, and lectures given in the Hall amused and informed town residents for decades.

Rural in character and far from busy Boston, Winchester in the 1850s and 1860s was still a relatively quiet village with a lazy, easy-paced atmosphere. Indians occasionally visited, camping on the open space in front of the church and selling baskets and fancy articles. Because of the growing commuter population, there was little activity during the day, and less community spirit, perhaps, than in towns where citizens both lived and worked. But some Winchester citizens, concerned about the lack of spirit, made efforts to enliven the town. Growth and prosperity were big concerns in post-Civil War America, and Winchesterites were as eager as any in the country to appear progressive. Auctioneers advertising real estate mentioned the town's beauty, taste, healthy atmosphere, and rail service, but not its peace and quiet. What we now see as a virtue in a town, "progressive" citizens feared in the mid-1800s. When the Boston and Lowell Railroad raised its fares in the late 1850s, there was widespread concern that the rise would discourage people from settling in Winchester and cause those already here to move out. But those fears were not realized; the village's population rose steadily and the proportion of commuters actually increased. The value of the town's real estate rose from $700,000 in 1850 to $1,250,000 ten years later. Winchester was well on its way to becoming a residential suburb.

The new technology of that progressive age certainly must have provided some excitement. Those years saw the introduction of many new inventions to Winchester, including the town's first public telegraph, located in Lyceum Hall, in 1866, and gas lamps on Main Street in 1864. The Congregational Church, Lyceum Hall, the train depot, and a few stores and residences had gaslight, but kerosene lit most houses until after 1880. The Lyceum offered frequent lectures on electricity, inventions, and other scientific topics. The railroad was still a novelty in the 1850s, and some country dwellers walked miles to watch the train pass. The railroad expanded the ordinary person's world and amazed him with its size and speed. One contemporary diarist noted with wonder how his father traveled from Winchester to Lowell in thirty minutes, a trip that would have taken hours by horse or canalboat.

But the town learned that technology could be a mixed blessing. The noise and pollution of the railroad and early industry made the Center a less desirable place in which to live, and areas around the grade

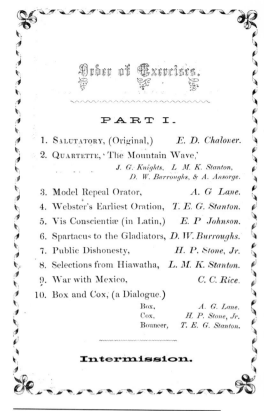

Before construction of the Town Hall, the Lyceum building was the cultural and civic meeting place for Victorian Winchesterites. This "Order of Exercise" shows a typical entertainment program of the time, this one presented by the Winchester Literary Association on New Year's Eve, 1857, 7 P.M. to midnight. Scarcely out with a bang.

The first electric light in Winchester was installed in a private home at 379 Main Street.

crossing such as Vine Street Hill and Shore Road, once popular residential locations, gradually became commercial. Owners converted homes into stores, or subdivided their houses and rented apartments to industrial workers. The prosperous of the town moved farther out Main, Church, and Washington Streets, away from the Center. But Elmwood Avenue, perhaps because of its position at the edge of the Center, remained a street for the well-to-do, and survived the Center's industrial phase. From 1865, Samuel S. Richardson lived at 18 Elmwood (torn down in 1984), and Asa Fletcher, the philanthropist after whom Fletcher Street was named, lived at 25–27 Elmwood in the 1870s. Other town center residences included Boston mayor F. O. Prince's summer house at 51 Vine Street, and two outstanding examples of early architecture that date from the mid 1800s—the Parker House, now at 60 Lloyd and formerly on the corner of Main and Mystic Valley Parkway, Winchester's finest example of the Italian Villa style, and the Oliver Gardner House, now at 5 Myrtle Street and formerly on the site of the Town Hall. The Gardner house, one of two identical Gothic Revival cottages that stood on the site of the town hall, was moved to Myrtle Street in 1887, when Oliver Gardner sold his portion of the land to the town. Its twin, which belonged to lumberyard owner Alexis Cutting, remained near the town

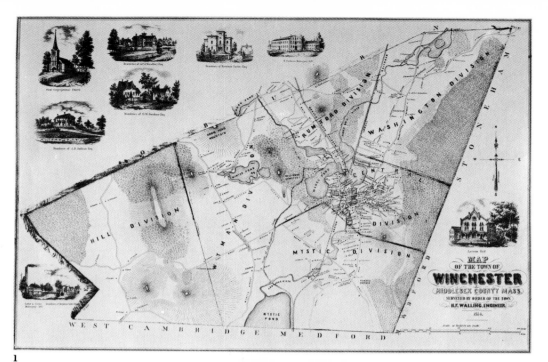

1

Though most prosperous Winchester residents ultimately moved their homes to neighborhoods out Church, Main, and Washington Streets, for some the Center remained *the* place to live. Among them were the Parkers and Gardners, whose important homes were illustrated on the 1854 map of Winchester residential areas; the Cuttings of lumberyard fame (photo 2); and Edmund Sanderson, a prominent merchant (photo 3).

2

Emergence of a True Victorian Town: Winchester Neighborhoods, 1830–1916

hall until 1968 when it was demolished to allow the Winchester Public Library to expand. One particularly interesting feature of the Gardner house is the ornate vergeboard along the inside of each steeply pitched gable. These patterns were cut with the newly invented jigsaw—a good example of how architecture can be influenced by new technology.

But generally the Center is noted for its commercial rather than residential buildings. Even the workers who lived there tended to move north with industry as the century progressed, though a cluster of worker houses at Winchester Place did manage to resist commercial development. Built between the 1840s and 1880s, the houses stand today as a remnant of early industry, a little island of vernacular homes amidst stores and offices.

Winchester continued to grow, passing from the status of a village to that of a town as businessmen, professionals, shopkeepers, and industrial workers moved in at a steady rate. During the 1870s citizens looked for the civic conveniences and necessities of town life, and, more important, provided the leadership and community spirit that brought

Expansion of the fire department after a rash of destructive fires led to the building of a new fire station on Winchester Place. In 1912 the town bought its first motorized piece of fire-fighting equipment, a "Knox Combination A."

them to realization. In November of 1870 the town chose a committee to consider how Winchester might gain its own water supply. The committee's reports started a process that culminated in the building of the town's reservoirs in the 1870s and 1880s. In 1871 the school initiated a curriculum change that marked the beginning of the use of modern educational methods in Winchester, and by 1880 the school system was firmly established and well conducted. In 1875 the town appropriated $750 to improve the town common; by 1882 the Village Improvement Association had started work that helped change the character of the Center. In 1871 and 1872 a series of disastrous fires, including one that destroyed the Whitney mill, convinced the townspeople that its old hand engine was inadequate, and in January 1873 the town bought a new steam engine that remained in service for forty years. The firefighting force expanded and the town built a new firehouse on Winchester Place. In 1878 the town selectmen appointed Winchester's first official chief-of-police, Zanoni Richardson, though for years he and his force had little to do but suppress the sale of illicit liquor and investigate the occasional burglary. Winchester was an expanding town, but it was also a safe one.

All of these civic developments took place without a town hall. In 1850 Colonel Winchester had asked that his $3000 gift to the town "be appropriated to the erection of a town hall or any other proper object of municipal expenditure." But a committee formed to research the matter reported that the hall would cost two and a half times that amount, and the town backed down. It simply didn't have the money, and besides, Asa Locke and others planned to build Lyceum Hall, which had plenty of rooms for town meetings and municipal offices. But by 1885 the Lyceum could hold only a third of the town's qualified voters. Town offices were inconveniently scattered all over the Center, and a heavy portion of the budget was used to rent municipal office space in the Brown and Stanton Block and other privately owned premises. Recognizing that a centrally located civic building was now an absolute necessity, in March the town formed a committee to consider the subject, and a year later voted to purchase the Gardner/Cutting lot on the corner of Washington and Mt. Vernon Streets. The decision generated a good deal of controversy when Gardner and Cutting asked what many thought was too much for their land. But town opinion was adamant, and after a series of heated debates by various committees, the town appropriated $50,000 for the building's construction. In March and December of 1887 a further $20,000 was appropriated to build and furnish a library extension. The town dedicated the structure at 71 Mt. Vernon Street on October 20, 1888.

Winchester now had a stately, distinctive, and serviceable civic center. Selectmen, board members, and other town officers moved into the new town hall. The chief of police and his patrolmen established offices there and built a new lock-up in the basement. (The old lock-up was at the firehouse on Vine Street, where a trial judge also held hearings; after 1873 Winchester was attached to the Woburn District Court, and the town hall was not needed for judicial proceedings.) The police department operated out of the town hall until 1914, when the town erected the L-shaped fire and police station at the corner of Mt. Vernon Street and Winchester Place. The library, which has a continuous history in

Winchester from 1848, remained in the east wing of the town hall until 1931, when Robert Coit designed the Gothic Revival style public library on Washington Street.

The Winchester town hall is perhaps the most architecturally significant structure in the town—a classic nineteenth-century American public building. The distinguished Boston architectural firm of Rand and Taylor designed it, incorporating popular ideas of the period and embodying in its construction the spirit of change that turned Winchester from an industrial village into a prosperous suburb. Like the old Winchester Savings Bank, the town hall reflects the influence of the famous nineteenth-century architect Henry Hobson Richardson. Richardson was one of America's most innovative architects, a man who brought European training and original thinking to a country with relatively little architectural tradition. Fortunately for Massachusetts, he chose Boston as his home and designed more than thirty public buildings in the metropolitan area, including Trinity Church in Boston and the Winn Memorial

Town Hall (photo courtesy of the Society for the Preservation of New England Antiquities).

Library in Woburn. Most of his work shows an interest in interlocking geometric shapes and the influence of the medieval architecture of France, Spain, and Italy, both of which characterize the town hall.

The hall contains many features of what is now called *Richardson Romanesque:* a heavy red stone surface, arched entryways and windows, Queen Anne-style rotundas, and asymmetrical facades. By the time the town appropriated the money for the library extension, the architects had already drawn the main plans, and though they incorporated many Richardsonian features in the extension, many townspeople thought it took away from the compactness of the whole. The angled roof, the placement of windows near the roof, and the large arched window on the exposed side of the extension are all features borrowed from Richardson's Law School at Harvard, which he designed in 1881. The clock tower, which was nominally financed by Colonel Winchester's thirty-eight-year-old gift, is a Winchester landmark. Though the interior of the building has changed considerably over the years, the exterior has not. Appropriately, the Massachusetts Historical Commission placed this exceptional building on the National Register of Historic Places in 1983.

Winchester built its town hall during perhaps the most important decade in its early history, the decade in which the town fully realized its identity as a residential suburb. In the decades that followed, the town experienced its most intense period of growth. From 1890 to 1910, Winchester's population rose from 5,000 to 10,000, and its assessed valuation from $4.5 million to nearly $13 million. The increase was almost wholly residential; industrially, the town had stood still. In the 1880s, much of what characterized a modern suburb emerged: the first newspaper, the first electric lights, plans for the first sewer system, the first trolleys. Indeed, much of the prosperity of the Center after 1890 was due to the introduction of a complex streetcar system. The first trolleys appeared in 1886, when the North Woburn Horse Railroad extended its tracks along Main Street from Woburn to Symmes Corner; in 1888 the company extended the line to the Medford border to meet a line that came up from Medford Square. At first, horses drew the trolleys and filled the town with the distinctive jingling of bridle bells, but in 1896 the company installed electric cars. The service lasted until the Eastern Massachusetts Railway introduced buses in 1928.

A less tangible but equally important element in the emergence of modern Winchester was the attitude of the town, or the image it had of itself. We have already seen how the town moved industry out of the Center during this period and beautified the parks and streets. These actions were part of a larger consciousness that the town developed as the century came to a close. The citizenry now had an idea of Winchester as residential, traditional, and prosperous. Planting trees and worrying about pollution were ingredients in a vision of the town's possibilities. And, as is so often the case during the flowering of an awareness of the present, there was a renewed interest in the past, spurred in part by the nation's centennial, 1876. Townspeople formed historical societies, studied family trees, and researched the history of town landmarks like the Middlesex Canal and the Congregational Church. In 1885 they celebrated the fiftieth anniversary of the railroad and published its history in local papers. Family reunions became popular, and the Richardsons, Carters, and others held large gatherings that attracted relatives from all over the United States and Canada. In 1855, amateur historians, including Nathaniel Richardson and Abijah Thompson, formed the Winchester Historical and Genealogical Society. It researched and presented a variety of papers and published its work in the *Winchester Record,* still one of the best sources of town history available.

By examining its past, Winchester defined its present. The depth of the town's roots, the continuity of its family histories, the contributions of new arrivals, and the knowledge that the town had always controlled its own destiny—all helped the people of the 1880s and 1890s to create and fulfill their vision of modern Winchester.

Chapter 2

Out Church Street: Development of the Suburban Ideal

The west side of Winchester was slow to develop. Main Street and Washington Street, which ran through the Center, had benefited directly from the industrial and commercial potential of the Aberjona River and the Boston and Lowell Railroad. Church Street, on the other hand, had always been a connecting road, passing through farmland and market gardens until well into the nineteenth century. In 1851, only three houses stood along its mile of length between the Center and Cambridge Street. But by the turn of the century, the pattern of residential development in the town, and the place of Winchester in the Boston metropolitan area, had changed significantly. Winchester had become a fine suburb, and the area west of the Center, on either side of Church Street, reflected the development of the affluent Victorian suburb better than any other part of town.

In the nineteenth century, urban migration and industrial development radically transformed American cities. As commerce took second

place to manufacturing, and hundreds of thousands of European immigrants and ex-farmers provided a pool of labor for industry, the country's municipalities grew rapidly and steadily. Throughout the United States and particularly along the North Atlantic seaboard, the change was dramatic and permanent. Boston, for example, grew from a small harbor town of 18,000 in 1790 to a sprawling city of a half-million in less than a century.

Unfortunately, the rapid urban growth created problems that the laws of the time were not equipped to handle. Zoning regulations and subdivision controls did not appear in the United States until after World

War I. The provision of public utilities, the maintenance of law and order, and the regulation of housing and commerce became increasingly difficult to effect. Cities became grim and congested. Vast slums sprang up. For the rising class of businessmen, professionals, and small manufacturers who benefited from urbanization, the city was a place in which to work, but not to live. These men and their families created a demand that the suburb supplied.

As an 1881 Boston newspaper put it, the suburb was "the golden mean between city and country." It provided the nouveau riche with fresh air, greenery, and quiet in a location easily accessible to the excitement and commerce of the city. Suburban housing reflected the status and wealth of the new professionals. Improved transportation made it possible to live and work in entirely different regions. The suburb was the turn-of-the-century answer to overcrowding and unpleasant surroundings—at least for the middle class. American urban planners kept pace with industrial and business growth by developing "green belts" around the huge cities. Influenced by experiments with "garden cities" and estate developments in England, these people started a pattern of metropolitan planning that was to change completely the structure of American residential life in the twentieth century.

Winchester, of course, had been a suburb of sorts since the 1830s. After the railroad opened up the area, many Boston businessmen built houses in the Center or on the Mystic Lakes and commuted to work. But it was not until the 1870s that the concept of the estate or suburban development blossomed. Typically, this was a group of houses built by an individual or syndicate, often financed by investors, and sold or rented to members of the rising middle class who were attracted to Winchester by its beauty and proximity to Boston, but who couldn't afford to build their own homes. The last three decades of the nineteenth century saw an unprecedented number of houses go up—to such an extent that in 1902 the *Winchester Star* reported that "the overbuilding of homes the past dozen years has caused enormous losses to investors and left hundreds of purchasers in debt." But the newspaper's bleak outlook was premature. In spite of the ups and downs of the trade, building continued at a healthy rate, and this period turned out to be one of the most important in the architectural history of the town.

Fortunately, the expansion of Winchester as a Victorian suburb coincided with the emergence of the town's self-identity. Between 1880 and 1910 the town moved industry to the north end and beautified the Center, and in this spirit town leaders also kept close watch on suburban building, making sure no unsightly development marred Winchester's beauty. In the absence of zoning laws, prominent citizens kept a careful eye on land ownership. Whenever the threat of overdevelopment occurred, some philanthropic town resident stepped in and saved the day with a timely purchase. Private enterprise and town government worked together, and though there was occasional conflict between town factions, suburban expansion went smoothly.

Because Church Street developed so slowly, by the time the idea of the suburb reached its zenith in the 1880s and 1890s, the land around it was still relatively empty. Close to the Center and free of woods and marshes, the prime flat land of Wyman's Plains was ideal for estate development. The developers who took advantage of this land were mostly Winchester residents who wanted to build quality houses for the upper-middle class. As a result, this area now contains some of the finest examples of late-Victorian suburbiana in the Boston area. Four developments stand out, each different in conception and style: Rangeley, a private park built by David N. Skillings; Wedgemere, a syndicate-built development of the 1890s; the Firth Development, a suburban retreat designed by Robert Coit; and Everett Avenue, a remarkable, wealthy residential area with an outstanding assortment of houses, most of which were designed by the Winchester architect Dexter Blaikie. The individual developments blend together beautifully, but they also show diversity in purpose and style. Though many houses were built in these neighborhoods after the original estates were completed, these four developments provided a foundation that gave the west side unity and made it into one of the most beautiful sections of Winchester.

Rangeley

In 1865 David N. Skillings bought five acres of land between the railroad and Church Street known at the time as "Collins Woods." This purchase marked the beginning of Rangeley, an estate that developed in the last quarter of the nineteenth century and represented, as much as any section of Winchester, the transformation from industrial town to upper-middle class suburb. Expensive, elitist, and architecturally impressive, Rangeley was an excellent example of the power of private enterprise in Winchester town planning. Three wealthy, philanthropic businessmen shaped the estate's growth and controlled its population: Skillings, his son-in-law Elisha Bangs, and the publishing mogul Edwin Ginn. Because of their efforts, Skillings's five acres grew into a substantial development filling out the triangle of land bordered by Church Street, Bacon Street, and the railroad tracks.

After Skillings bought Collins Woods, he cleared much of its timber, bought additional land to the south, and slowly transformed the region into a charming park-like estate. His intentions were two-fold. Obviously, he developed the area as a personal investment. But Skillings, always active in town improvements, was also eager to establish a park that the whole community could appreciate. Before he bought the land it was a rough tract of uneven ground covered with dense vegetation and swamps. A dilapidated tenement house swarming, as one newspaper put it, "with a low class of people" sat there in full view of Church Street. By buying and improving the property, Skillings "removed a blot from the landscape that might have spread and changed the character of the entire locality."

All this was true, but the elitist tone of these newspaper remarks suggests an ambiguity. On the one hand, Skillings was doing the community a service by improving a "gravelly waste" so close to the town center. On the other hand, he was moving toward the establishment of a private park on a prime piece of property. Ironically, the estate eventually catered only to his family and friends, in spite of his original intentions. Skillings owned the property, of course, and was free to do with it as he wished, but he also exercised his considerable political power to the benefit of his real estate plans. Taxes on the property were always lower than some of the less-privileged in the town thought fair, and controversy over the accessibility and tax-status of the estate continued for decades after Skillings's death in 1880. Without questioning his motives, which appeared always to be honest and generous, it is probably fair to say that there was plenty of room in Skillings's purchase and development of Rangeley for both philanthropy and personal gain.

Not that Skillings was an aristocrat or elitist himself. From humble beginnings in his native state of Maine, he came to his position of wealth and influence gradually, working by turns as a carpenter, a newspaperman, a builder, and a coal and wood merchant. By the time he moved from Boston to Winchester in 1854, he was head of a large lumber firm with branches in Vermont and Michigan. He became well-known in Winchester for his generosity, integrity, and civic-mindedness. He was a deacon in the Congregational Church, a strong prohibitionist, a town selectman for three years and water commissioner for five, and a representative in the state legislature. He led the fight for the reservoir system and helped found the Village Improvement Association. Like Forrest Manchester, he used his money, influence, and unflagging energy to bring a particular vision of the town to life. An important element in that vision was the development of Rangeley.

Skillings began by razing the tenement and building his own mansion on a knoll at the center of the estate. Broad, sweeping lawns and groves of natural forest surrounded the house, which stood behind the present 9 Rangeley Road. Unfortunately, later owners tore the mansion down in 1933, but the estate stable, converted to a residence, still stands at 19 Rangeley. After completing his mansion, Skillings built a number of fine houses that he rented to specific friends and relatives that he wanted as neighbors. In 1876 he completed three fine examples of the Queen Anne–panel brick style: 2–4 Rangeley, 38 Rangeley, and 9 Meadowcroft Road. Some of Winchester's most prominent nineteenth-century residents occupied these houses, including, at 38 Rangeley, Samuel Elder, a prominent Boston attorney who acted as counsel to the U.S. government at the Fisheries Arbitration Case at the Hague. Skillings ensured his tenants' privacy by building a solid, costly stone wall along the entire frontage of the estate on Church Street. Later in the 1870s he built more houses on Rangeley Road, including numbers 14, 22, 26, and 37. These too went to "hand-picked buyers." By carefully choosing his neighbors and separating them from the rest of town, Skillings kept firm control of his community within a community.

When Skillings died in 1880 the estate passed into the control of

From humble beginnings, David N. Skillings created a controversial and prestigious "private park" in the area known as Rangeley. His own "mansion house" there (right) was torn down in 1933; another beautiful Skillings estate, that of David Jr., once stood on Mt. Vernon Street opposite Town Hall, but it too is lost.

his son, D. Nelson Skillings, and his son-in-law, Elisha Bangs, who had married Georgiana Skillings in 1871. President of the Boston Stock Exchange, Bangs was a shrewd speculator who fully recognized the value of Skillings's plans. Bangs maintained the estate as a private park and continued development. He built his own mansion on Central Green, put up houses on Central Street, and built Rangeley Hall, a lively social club that featured musical events and theatrical entertainments. The "Back Log Club" flourished for over twenty years, until the hall's demolition in 1905. During the day the hall served as a community school, and Mary Winsor, who later established the prestigious School for Girls in Boston, had her first teaching assignment here.

But it was only a matter of time before the majority of townspeople, resentful of the social and physical exclusiveness of this private park near the center of town, began to complain. Many people made a point of using the streets of Rangeley as freely as they would any city street. The owners countered, as this item from the July 2, 1885 *Woburn Journal* attests:

> Notices have been posted in Rangeley that all persons except
> tenants are forbidden to pass through it for any purpose whatever.
> Although the owners have a perfect right to do it, yet it seems hard
> that these beautiful grounds should be debarred to outsiders who wish
> to use it merely as a thoroughfare.

Some townspeople were angry. The following evening, vandals broke
gaslights, upset vases, and did other damage to the estate. Those responsible were delinquent, but this action did reflect a deeper dissatisfaction.
In September there was further trouble. Residents of Rangeley complained about "gangs of hoodlums" who would "roost on the stone wall
in front of Rangeley nights and insult ladies as they passed." Though
these gangs were no doubt nothing more than idle teen-agers passing
the evening hours away, their choice of the wall at Rangeley as a hangout
was perhaps significant. A physical manifestation of the estate's exclusiveness, the wall provided a focus for the boys' resentment, which mirrored that of the town.

In the 1890s the issue of taxation added to the controversy. Town
opinion divided between those who thought the estate was not taxed
enough, and those who felt that estates like Rangeley were, as the *Winchester Star* put it, "public parks maintained at the expense of the owners." Henry F. Johnson, a frequent contributor to the *Star,* was a leading
advocate of increased taxation. Edwin Ginn, who owned a large estate
himself just south of Rangeley, argued in letters to the paper that attractive estates were of great benefit to the town.

The issue raged for years, but changed complexion at the turn of
the century. A team of runaway horses knocked Bangs down in the
streets of Winchester and he soon contracted tetanus and died. The heirs
of the estate could not afford to keep Rangeley in its park-like form, and
had to sell to a Boston developer who planned to subdivide the estate
into a hundred house lots. When the town heard of these plans it became
united; as much as the townspeople disliked the elitism of Rangeley,
they feared even more the prospect of a crowded development that would
"drive many of our best citizens from town." In November of 1901, the
Star printed a long piece on "The Passing of Rangeley," and came down
solidly on the side of limited taxation. When Edwin Ginn came to the
rescue in 1902 by buying back the estate from the Boston developer, he

parlayed this sentiment to his own advantage, convincing town leaders that the property, now enlarged to include his own estate on Ginn Road, was overtaxed. Mr. Ginn got his lower taxes and the town got a Rangeley that retained its unique, park-like character.

Ginn was a worthy successor to Skillings and Bangs. Though he never involved himself in politics, he managed to exert tremendous influence in the town. He was instrumental in the creation of Manchester Field and deeded some of his own land to the Metropolitan Park Commission when the commission established the parkway system in the 1890s. In 1902 he proposed that Winchester establish a Village Improvement Society to oversee low-income housing in the town. A strong pacifist, he was elected president of the World Peace Federation board of trustees in 1910. In 1914, shortly before he died, he left a million dollars to start the World Peace Foundation, still in existence today. It was appropriate that Rangeley ended up in his hands. He was typical of the kind of nineteenth-century man who shaped Winchester: self-made, philanthropic, strong-willed, conservative, generous, and not above using his wealth and power when the good of the town demanded it.

Rangeley marked the opening up of Winchester's west side. Though hardly an average development, the estate did set the tone for further suburban growth. Later developers of the area followed Skillings's example by building high-quality houses in rural surroundings for prosperous residents. When suburban planning reached the peak of its early popularity late in the century, planners found they had a perfect model right in their neighborhood.

Wedgemere Syndicate and the Firth Development

But the developers came slowly. Apart from Rangeley, the land on either side of Church Street remained largely undeveloped before 1890. A few houses dotted the landscape, but Wymans Plains had more farms and market gardens than residences. As late as 1889, Church, Bacon, Fletcher, Central, and Wildwood Streets were the only roads between the center and Cambridge Street.

WINCHESTER
MIDDLESEX COUNTY
MASS. 1886.

In the 1880s, while Elisha Bangs developed Central Street, some prominent Boston businessmen built houses on Wildwood Street in a variety of Victorian architectural styles. The well-known florist Samuel Twombly, who owned three houses and a good deal of land on Wildwood Street, lived in a Greek Revival house built on Cambridge Street in the 1850s and moved to its present location at 93 Wildwood some

Land on both sides of Church Street remained largely undeveloped well into the late nineteenth century, as seen in this 1886 map of Winchester.

Emergence of a True Victorian Town: Winchester Neighborhoods, 1830–1916

time in the 1880s. Twombly also owned the house at 36 Wildwood and the handsome Richardsonian house at 25, built by the Boston and Maine Railroad executive William Berry in 1886. The Boston lawyer John T. Wilson, who was often called upon to moderate town meetings in Winchester's early years, built and rented out the Italianate houses at 5 and 7 Wildwood Street in 1876. And at 1 Wildwood, John Rhodes built a Queen Anne–style home. Rhodes, a Boston broker and busy socialite, brought the street to the attention of the town by composing a polka he named "Wildwood," which he performed at one of the annual balls of the Calumet Club.

But the development of Wildwood Street was the exception, not the rule. Most of the west-side streets appeared as part of the developments that sprang up after 1890, when the suburbs were the rage in Boston. City planners and public leaders envisaged a green belt around the Hub stretching from Lynn in the north to the Blue Hills in the south, and from Winthrop in the east to Waltham in the west. Winchester figured prominently in informal discussions of this scheme. The town had gained a substantial reputation in its short life, and Boston newspapers and magazines frequently noted its qualities: proximity to Boston, excellent architecture, beautiful streets, and good civic spirit. Real estate agents used Rangeley as an example of tasteful development. In 1881, the *Boston Herald* compared Winchester to Bedford Park, a unique garden suburb of London noted for its progressive mix of architectural styles. All this attention caused developers to look to Winchester just at the time when affordable middle class housing was needed.

H. H. Richardson, the Brookline-based architect whose ideas influenced the designers of the town hall and the first Winchester Savings Bank building, wrote often in the 1880s about the need for suburban housing for the rising professional class. Richardson suggested that houses that concentrated on "form and proportion;" that dispensed with "all superfluous ornamentation;" and that used less surrounding land than most country houses, could be built at a price that would allow their owners to rent them for $200 to $500 a year. In Winchester two development projects, the Wedgemere Syndicate and the Firth Development, provided this kind of housing—although rents, as one would expect for Winchester, tended to be at the upper end of Richardson's scale.

Typical of middle-class suburban housing in 1898 was the home of Mrs. Samuel Symmes at 7 Sanborn Street.

Emergence of a True Victorian Town: Winchester Neighborhoods, 1830–1916

Influenced by Rangeley's success, a Winchester realtor named Frank Forsyth conceived the idea of forming a land syndicate to develop the Wymans Plains area on the north side of Church Street. He founded the West Side Syndicate, which bought up the land from Church Street to as far north as Wildwood Cemetery and as far west as Cambridge Street. The land there was very flat, and the syndicate laid out streets on a grid extending over 75 acres, including Calumet Road; Foxcroft Road; Salisbury, Oxford, Yale, and Cabot Streets; and Wedgemere Avenue. The syndicate changed its name to the Wedgemere Syndicate; sold stocks to Boston investors; subdivided the land into uniform parcels; and started to build.

For the first few years the syndicate did very well, but the financial panic of 1893 slowed the venture, and two years later the owners sold out—in most cases to the banks that had advanced the mortgage money. For a few years building all but came to a halt, but by 1898 construction was again in full swing. Builders put up over 90 houses on the seven principal streets of Wedgemere between 1890 and 1916, including some excellent examples of three late Victorian architectural styles—Tudor, Colonial Revival, and Queen Anne. As a result, the district has a historical importance and an architectural integrity unusual for a development of this size. Some of Winchester's most prominent developers, including George Whitehorne and Phineas Nickerson, built houses on Wedgemere's streets. Although the district scarcely conforms to our twentieth-century notion of a development, it is an excellent example of what careful planning and workmanship can produce.

Another west-side development from this period, smaller in scope than the Wedgemere Syndicate but just as impressive in its architecture, is the Firth Development. In 1890, William and Isabella Firth bought a large estate between Church Street and Wedge Pond, and moved into the old Charles Curtis House at 11 Grassmere Road. Curtis, who owned an estate on nearby Curtis Street, had built this beautiful house in 1865. One of Winchester's few Gothic Revival cottages, the house has some lovely features, including deep eaves with gingerbread vergeboard and stained glass.

Between 1896 and 1899, the Firths laid out Glengarry and Grassmere Roads and divided their estate into modest house lots. They hired

WEDGEMERE PARK,
WINCHESTER, MASS.

Scale 160 feet to an inch.

June, 1891.

NOTE. AREAS AND DISTANCES ON THIS PLAN
ARE APPROXIMATE ONLY.

CROSS SECTION OF AVENUES.

SCALE 16 FEET TO AN INCH.

D. W. Pratt,
Resident Engineer.

Emergence of a True Victorian Town: Winchester Neighborhoods, 1830–1916

The Wedgemere neighborhood of town is the product of a turn-of-the-century real estate investment syndicate: a suburban development. The project spanned more than twenty-five years and yielded more than ninety examples, many of them fine, of the most popular late-Victorian house styles.

Boston architect and Winchester resident Robert Coit, whose work included the Winchester Boat Club, to design attractive middle–class houses. Using Coit's designs, which combined Colonial Revival, Tudor, and Queen Anne styles, the Firths built ten houses on Glengarry Road, one on Grassmere Road, and three on Dix Street, all during the 1890s. William Firth placed advertisements in Boston newspapers, describing the houses as "situated in the best part of Winchester, five minutes from steam and five minutes from electric cars." Rents ranged from $575 to $625 per year, rather high for the time. Various professional and business people rented the houses, including a shoe manufacturer, a banker, and a fishnet maker. Laid out on the rolling ground near Wedge Pond, the Firth Development had a variety and charm rare in any but the most sophisticated suburbs. The only clue to its modest origins is the small size of the lots; otherwise, the development is an outstanding example of the Victorian garden suburb.

Everett Avenue

Everett Avenue is one of Winchester's prime residential areas. On a gently curving street overlooking the Mystic Lakes, some of Winchester's finest houses exhibit a broad range of architectural styles. With the side streets Stratford Road, Sheffield Road, and Sheffield West, Everett Avenue is so distinguished that the word development scarcely seems appropriate. These streets were not middleclass—they attracted the wealthy. As the *Winchester Star* said frankly in 1914, "substantial, commodious houses in this physically attractive location on lakefront property make this area desirable and a symbol of success."

The street was named after Edward Everett, a renowned scholar and orator who was president of Harvard, governor of Massachusetts, member of the United States Senate, and candidate for the vice presidency. He bought land from Deacon Luke Wyman in 1858 and built a 21-room house for his son Everett on the Mystic Lakes at the foot of Myopia Hill; Robinson Park now runs through his old estate. During the Civil War, when the city of Charlestown built a dam between the two Mystic Lakes and caused the water level of the upper lake to rise, Everett claimed that the change spoiled the estate. He sued the city of Charlestown and won, though he had died by the time of the settlement.

Everett Avenue began as a private way connecting the Cole House, now 8 Everett, to Bacon Street. Joseph Foxcroft Cole was a famous landscape painter, one of many artists drawn to Winchester by its natural beauty. Attracted by the excellent view of the lake, he built his Colonial Revival house here in 1878.

But fifteen years passed before a second house appeared on the avenue. In 1893 the architect Dexter Blaikie built a Tudor residence for himself at number 45. Blaikie saw the area's potential and soon planned more houses. Building began in 1896, and over the next 20 years about 70 houses went up along Everett Avenue and its three new side roads. Though some of Boston's finest architects, including Robert Coit and F. Patterson Smith, designed several of the houses, the key men behind the development were Blaikie and his associate Phineas Nickerson.

Blaikie came from a family of architects—his brothers Edwin and William designed the old Winchester Savings Bank. Dexter was already building in Winchester when Nickerson, a retired sea captain, moved there in 1894. Nickerson liked Blaikie's houses and asked him to be his builder. Together they helped transform the west side, erecting sound, well-designed stucco houses on Church Street, in Wedgemere, and most of all throughout the Everett Avenue district. Over a third of the 70 houses in the district were products of the Blaikie-Nickerson collaboration. They gave the area its distinctive character.

The district contains good examples of almost every turn-of-the-century architectural style. The Tudor style, very popular at the time, is well-represented. Both Blaikie and Nickerson lived in Tudor houses, 45 Everett and 93 Church, respectively, and in 1911 they built a fine example of the style at 23 Sheffield Road. Number 34 Everett Avenue is a beautiful Mediterranean-style house and 11 Sheffield West is one of Winchester's few true bungalows. There are also excellent examples of the Shingle and Queen Anne styles, and some of the town's most impressive Colonial Revival houses, including the Hilton House at 3 Stratford Road. It is in large part this mix of interesting styles that prevents this very methodically developed area from appearing to be a development.

Prominent business and professional people bought these houses. Daniel Beggs, president of the Beggs and Cobb Tannery, lived at 2 Everett Avenue; Roland Sherman, town attorney after 1919, lived at 14 Everett Avenue; Oren Sanborn, son of the founder of the Chase and Sanborn Coffee Company, lived in a Blaikie-Nickerson house at 12 Sheffield Road until he built his mansion on High Street in 1907. Everett Chadwick, the patent attorney who obtained the original patent for the Gillette Safety Razor, lived in a Colonial Revival house at 24 Everett Avenue designed by F. Patterson Smith. Smith was a well-known architect who designed the Winchester Country Club on Cambridge Street and the Church of the Epiphany on Mt. Vernon Street. Smith's first Winchester house was 30 Everett Avenue, designed in a style he created that was reminiscent of English country houses.

All of the district's houses fit in charmingly with each other and with the surrounding scenery. Everett Avenue is Winchester's finest expression of the turn-of-the-century interest in developing suburbs and beautifying cities. Like the other west-side developments, the Everett Avenue district has both unity and diversity: unity in its distinct feeling of neighborhood; diversity in its broad range of styles. Today, nearly a hundred years later, the area preserves its unique atmosphere.

As we saw in Part I, the hills west of Cambridge Street were still mostly farmland in 1916. This part of town did not attract developers until well into the twentieth century. But though the area was too rough and hilly for the early suburban developers, Myopia Hill did attract individual builders. The slopes of High Street, Fernway, and Arlington Street had privacy, beautiful woods, and fine views of the lakes, and some of the town's wealthiest citizens built their homes there. Samuel Elder, Governor Samuel McCall, and the piano manufacturer Handel Pond owned costly houses on Myopia Hill, and Jere Downes—nephew of Winchester's wealthy real estate brokers and builders, the Blank brothers—built the Jacobian Revival house at 1 Arlington Street.

But the most impressive residence in this area, if not the town, was the Oren Sanborn Mansion at 15 High Street. Sanborn built this magnificent structure in 1907 at the cost of quarter of a million dollars. A wonderful example of the Beaux Arts Classical Style, it is unlike anything else in Winchester; not even the town's public buildings match its grace and scope. Originally the main building had eighteen rooms and five bathrooms. The four-car garage was equipped with a turntable that saved drivers from having to back out the door. The gardens were extensive and opulent. The Sanborns were busy socialites who entertained frequently. "Aigremont," as the family called the mansion, was often the scene of elaborate parties in its large rooms or formal gardens until the family sold it in 1921. The new owner, Edward Downes, kept the tradition of social gatherings alive until 1947, when the Roman Catholic Church bought the mansion and turned it into a school. In 1968 the town acquired the building. Though less elegantly used than in its glory days, the mansion, which is listed in the National Register of Historical Places, still presides grandly from its position overlooking the town.

Chapter 3

Out Washington Street: Immigrants and Industrialization

In 1850 the northern part of Winchester was a broad, sparsely inhabited area of farmland, woods, and hills. From Horn Pond Brook in the west to the Middlesex Fells in the east, only a sprinkling of residences, farms, and small industries dotted the landscape. There were few roads. Main, Washington, Forest, and Cross Streets were the only accepted town ways. All other roads, including the beginnings of Oak Street and Swanton Street, were private ways, lanes laid by citizens to develop their property. Two branches of the Boston and Lowell Railroad ran through the region: one line roughly paralleled the Aberjona River; the other, Main Street. A few families owned most of the land—the Holtons, Stones, Fletchers, Cutters, and Richardsons. The Cutter family lived and worked in a concentration of houses north of Wedge Pond. Lane Funeral Service on Main Street now occupies an old Cutter house, built by Henry Cutter in 1845 and lying at the heart of what was once called Cutter Village. The Richardson family lived throughout the north

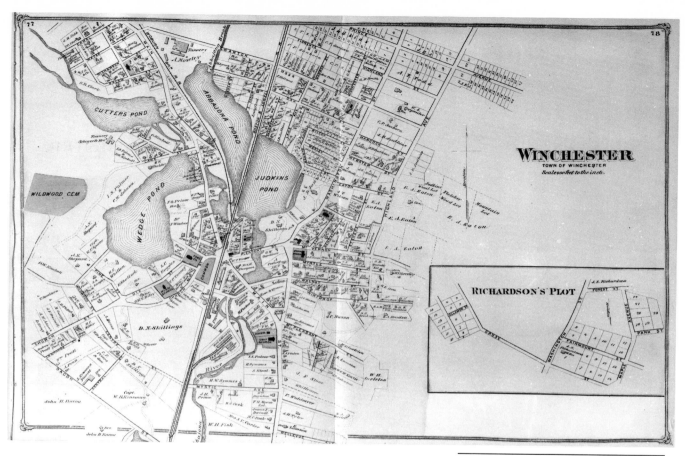

side, but the family's largest enclave was in the northeast corner of the town, where its members farmed and ran businesses along Forest Street and upper Washington Street. Today there are eight Richardson houses on Forest Street alone.

But the north side did not remain undeveloped for long. Soon after town incorporation, several enterprising individuals, including Jerome B. Judkins and Patrick Holland, bought up land and began to build houses and lay roads. These men saw the same suburban potential in the plains around Swanton Street and the gentle hills west of Washington Street that later developers recognized elsewhere in town. They knew that Winchester's future was as a residential town, and they wanted to stake an early claim in the housing market.

The Richardsons were one of a handful of families who dominated the North End of Winchester, and were prominent in the development of the town.

Emergence of a True Victorian Town: Winchester Neighborhoods, 1830–1916

Their vision, however, was a clouded one, and by 1870 it was clear that industry, not homes, was to be the distinctive characteristic of the region. Except for a thin slice of upper-middle-class housing that sprang up east of Washington Street in the late 1800s, the north end of town was distinctly working class for most of the latter half of the nineteenth century and the beginning of the twentieth. The particular flavor the area has today, with its worker housing, commercial enterprises, and vibrant ethnic mix, is a direct result of industrial growth. After the Civil War, the area bordering Washington Street, often called the *North End,* was almost synonymous with industry.

Part of the reason for this growth was the determined effort by nineteenth-century town leaders to move all industry out of Winchester Center. If Winchester was to develop as a residential suburb, it could not have the blight of industry within sight of the town common. With two railroad lines, excellent sources of waterpower at Horn Pond Brook and the Aberjona River, a number of operative mills, and a good deal of open space, the North End had a natural industrial infrastructure. The town map of 1854 shows a number of small industries already established: Church and Lane manufactured piano cases at the site of the old Belknap mill on Horn Pond Brook; the Cutters ran two mahogany mills, one on Wedge Pond and the other on the upper Aberjona River; and a small tannery did business next to the railroad line just south of Cross Street. In those days, the leather industry was growing quickly, and shoe shops lined Forest and Washington Streets. As the industry expanded, the North End was a natural spot for its factories, shops, and tanneries.

Until 1890, most heavy industry was leather related. Woburn was one of the biggest leather producers in Massachusetts, and Winchester, formerly part of Woburn, naturally followed. After the Civil War, currier shops, shoe shops, and factories that prepared leather for commercial use filled the North End. In the 1870s three large tanneries appeared: the Loring and Avery Tannery at the junction of Main and Swanton Streets in 1870, the Maxwell Tannery on Cross Street in 1872, and the Blank Brothers Tannery on Lake Street in 1879. Unlike the earlier, smaller industries, these factories changed the look of the North End dramatically. The buildings were large and ugly with protruding smokestacks and dull facades. They dumped waste into the river and streets and belched

1

2

Emergence of a True Victorian Town: Winchester Neighborhoods, 1830–1916

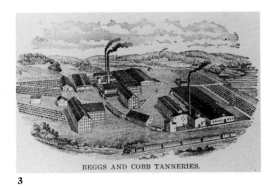

BEGGS AND COBB TANNERIES.

3

In tandem with the central neighborhoods' emergence as desirable residential areas, the North End developed into a flourishing commercial center. Among the large factories that thrived there in the late nineteenth century were (1) the McKay Metallic Fastener Company (United Shoe Machinery) on Washington Street, Puffer Manufacturing (which later took over the McKay building), (2) Cowdrey, Cobb, & Nichols (later Eastern Felt), and (3) the Beggs and Cobb Tannery.

smoke into the air. But they were also profitable and job-producing— by 1883 the three tanneries employed over 500 people. The Loring and Avery later became the Beggs and Cobb Tannery, the largest manufacturer of shoe-upper leather in the United States and the longest surviving leather company in Winchester, operating on Swanton Street, where the Parkview Apartments are now, until 1957.

While the Village Improvement Association beautified the town Center during the 1880s and 1890s, North End industry expanded and diversified. The McKay Metallic Fastener Company, which in its prime employed 1500 people, built a large factory on Swanton Street. The Eastern Felt Company, the Whitten Gelatine Company, the Puffer Manufacturing Company, and a host of smaller industries crowded onto the plains between Washington and Main Streets. By the turn of the century, Winchester industry in the North End employed thousands of people and generated millions of dollars' worth of manufactured goods. And all this development took place while Winchester emerged as a residential suburb!

The industrial development of the North End also transformed the ethnic composition of the town. Between 1860 and 1920, America's peak years of immigration, Winchester's ethnic character changed significantly. What had been an almost exclusively Yankee, native-born population was, by 1920, 40 percent foreign-born. Immigrants came from Canada, the Scandinavian countries, Greece, Armenia, Germany, Italy, and Ireland. The new arrivals settled all over Winchester, but the largest groups, the Irish and Italians, came to the North End, attracted by jobs and affordable housing. Gradually, the plains of Swanton developed into a distinct section of town that reflected the culture and concerns of these new residents.

The Irish were the first to arrive. They came as early as the 1850s, before heavy industry developed, and worked on the railroad, in small industry, and as servants in the town's wealthy homes. During the 1870s, the Irish population swelled to over 500, filling job openings in expanding industries as laborers, machinists, tanners, and curriers; many brought the skills of the leather trade with them from Ireland. Though some owned their own homes, most of the early Irish settlers lived in North End rental properties owned by banks or out-of-town investors.

The Irish had certain advantages over other immigrants that helped them to move quickly up the social scale, including native proficiency in English and early arrival in the country. Like their counterparts throughout the United States, many Winchester Irish found upward mobility through municipal service: town government, civil service, and the police and fire departments. Others made their way into business and professions. By 1920 the town had thoroughly assimilated the Irish, and many families could count back several generations of residence in Winchester. But there was little movement beyond the neighborhoods settled in the nineteenth century, and even today most Winchester Irish remain concentrated in the North End.

The main wave of Italian immigration came later, beginning at the turn of the century and slowing after 1924, the year of the U.S. Immigration Act. The Italian immigrants usually came to Winchester by way of Cambridge, Somerville, and Boston. Their numbers grew quickly: in the 1890s there were only three Italian families in Winchester; by 1915 there were hundreds, with a total population exceeding a thousand.

Like the Irish, the Italians brought skills from the old country. Most of the early Italian settlers were farmers, trained in an intensive farming suited to the fertile southern regions of their origin—Campania, Calabria, and Sicily. Their methods transferred well, and New England farmers appreciated their skills. The first Italians in Winchester worked on the Symmes farm, and by the turn of the century most of Winchester's farm workers were Italians. Later, many Italians ran their own market gardens, particularly around Swanton Street. Others worked in local construction companies and industries. Skilled stoneworkers made marble soda fountains for the Puffer Manufacturing Company, and cobblers and leather workers found jobs in shoe shops and tanneries.

Industry and immigration, then, shaped the North End. Catholic, blue collar, and ethnic, the area differed in almost every respect from the other, predominantly Yankee neighborhoods. These differences often created problems. The quality of life in the North End was significantly lower than in the rest of the town. Residents lived on crowded, polluted streets. The men worked 60-hour weeks in factories that were unsafe. Local newspapers of the 1880s and 1890s frequently reported lost fingers, crushed hands, and even loss of life, especially in the tanneries.

Industrial waste collected on the streets. The powerful and prosperous members of the community had little awareness of what it was like to work in a factory or live in a tenement, and the age of social reform had not yet arrived. So when North End residents complained of conditions at Town Meeting, little was done.

The barriers of religion and class also bred resentment. In the nineteenth century, social life was stratified and communication between the classes infrequent. North-Enders often saw west-side residents as a cliquish group that controlled the community for its own benefit. The west siders, in turn, often viewed the immigrants with prejudice and suspicion. There were also internal conflicts within the neighborhood. The Italians, as latecomers, faced resentment from the Irish and blacks who had been in the North End for decades. One black minister advised his parishioners not to sell their houses to Italians. The Italians resented Irish domination of the church.

But these kinds of problems were not unusual for a community undergoing vast changes in a short period, and tension, when it did surface, manifested itself in specific, minor issues such as the exclusiveness of Rangeley. As time passed, North-Enders became involved in business and politics, and successfully assimilated into the community. The town came to view ethnic diversity as an enrichment, and accepted the cultural gifts the immigrants had to offer. For years the Italian celebration of the Feast of the Assumption, with its pageantry, music, and fireworks, has been a favorite Winchester summer occasion.

During the 1920s and 1930s, heavy industry began to disappear from Winchester, forced out by economic circumstances, new zoning laws, and increased labor activity. But its influence on architecture in the North End can still be seen. Today there are two well-defined architectural districts with very different heritages. The main district west of Washington Street is where industry and immigration determined the pattern of housing and the kinds of houses built. Neighborhoods were sharply defined; houses were small and uniform in style. The area's factory workers and laborers, almost all of them Irish and Italian, lived here. East of Washington Street was developed after the turn of the century. Upper-middle-class citizens, including some who owned factories across Washington Street, built houses here. No Irish or Italian names appeared among home owners on this side of the street until well into the twentieth century. With a greater range of architectural styles, this much smaller section of the North End is closer in looks and atmosphere to the Victorian developments of the west side.

West of Washington Street

In 1854, three private ways connected Washington Street with the main line of the Boston and Lowell Railroad. These ways later became Swanton, Oak, and Nelson Streets. Of the eight houses on these ways, two belonged to Patrick Holland and Nicholas Fitzgerald, important figures in the history of Winchester's Irish-American community. These men were the first of a long line of Irish property owners, including Thomas Quigley, Dennis O'Connell, Edward Sullivan, and John Lyman, who developed the Swanton Street area into Winchester's first ethnic neighborhood.

The Irish developers were not speculators or real estate moguls, but ordinary working men who channelled their earnings back into the community by investing in property. Holland, for example, was a section boss and foreman on the railroad. He started investing in North End property in the 1850s when land there was still very cheap. By 1870, when Swanton Street had been extended across the tracks to join Main Street, Holland owned seven of the twenty houses on the street. By this time the area was almost entirely Irish, yet still on the threshhold of its greatest period of growth. From 1870 to 1900, when heavy industry dominated the North End and created hundreds of jobs, the Irish population swelled from under 400 to over 1,000.

Many of the new arrivals rented or bought houses in the Swanton Street neighborhood. Holland, the contractor Thomas Quigley, currier Dennis O'Connell, and the laborer Patrick Callaghan developed Oak Street, Westley Street, Holland Street, and Spruce Street (called Shamrock Street before 1897). They built simple, closely settled houses that the average laborer could afford. The row of architecturally similar cottages from 5 to 39 Nelson Street is an excellent and well-preserved example of a late-nineteenth-century worker development. John Lyman built its vernacular Queen Anne and Mansard houses in the 1890s for the Irish laboring class. These houses are typical of the area, but mixed in among them are a few larger, older houses, including the Francis H. Johnson house at 68 Nelson Street. In the 1880s Patrick Holland moved this house, formerly owned by the blacksmith who provided tie-bolts and ironmongery for the building of the railroad, from Main Street. He turned it into a tenant house and rented rooms to Irish laborers, teamsters, and factory workers.

In 1874, the establishment of St. Mary's Catholic Church on Washington Street gave impetus to the Irish settlement and focus to the growing sense of neighborhood. Businesses serving the community, including grocery stores, a hardware store, and a barbershop, sprang up along Swanton Street and lower Washington Street. At the corner of Swanton and Cedar Streets, John and Thomas Lynch opened a market that flourished until very recently. By the turn of the century the neighborhood was almost entirely Irish, and its residents had roots. Families often divided lots so that they could build houses for newlywed sons and daughters, or people chose houses that would allow them to be near their relatives. When St. Mary's acquired the Judkin's Estate in 1912 and built a new rectory and parochial school, the community was complete.

The Irish also settled the area north of Swanton Street, though most properties there originally belonged to out-of-towners. From the 1890s on, Irish workers rented houses along the newly opened Harvard and Irving Streets. But these two roads were also the center for Winchester's early black population. Between 1890 and 1920 over 200 blacks moved to Winchester, and in 1916 blacks owned nearly half of the 51 houses on Harvard and Irving, known then as the "checkerboard streets" because of their racial balance. Most of the blacks came from the agricultural South, driven off the land by mechanization. Like the Irish, they worked as servants, laborers, and tanners. Blacks, too, found a sense of community in their churches, especially the Hope Baptist Church. Founded by Reverend A. O. Smith in 1896, the Hope received permission from the town to use the old Washington schoolhouse at 12 Cross Street for its services. In 1907, the Reverend William Smith bought a house at 9 Harvard Street, in the heart of the black community, that he used as a parsonage for the church. The area remained a distinct black

Winchester Park

15 Minutes From BOSTON

The Finest Suburb of BOSTON Not a New Town But one already Established With all the Luxuries of Modern Civilization at your door

---

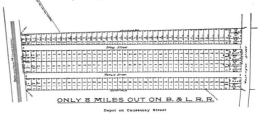

Winchester Park

ONLY 8 MILES OUT ON B. & L. R. R.

Depot on Causeway Street

. . Frequent Trains and quick time, only 15 minutes from Boston by express, makes this place nearer your business than most places in the city proper. This is not an isolated tract, away from any settlement, simply cut up "For Sale" but is near the centre of *Winchester*, Boston's model superb, with buildings upon all sides and with all modern improvements. Streets all made. Highland water. Electric Lights. Gas. Free Postal Deliveries daily. 2 Depots near.

. . House Lots from $150 up. only $5 to $10 down, $1 to $2 weekly. No interest, no taxes, no mortgage. In case of the death of the purchaser before paying for his lot, a deed will be given, free from all incumbrances without furthur payment. *Own a home.* "There is no place like home." It is within the reach of all. *Every lot desirable.* Convenient to schools. Public Library, churches, stores, etc.

. . No cash payment required if you build at once. After you have half paid for your lot, we will give deed, and take mortgage back if you prefer. *When your lot* is paid for, there is no trouble in getting a home. We will build a house on easy terms for any one who pays cash for their lot. *Several houses* will be built upon this land at once. *Building lines* established, securing uniform lawns in front of each house.

. . Buy and own a home. $5 to $10 down and $1 to $2 weekly will do it. You will not miss this small sum, and in a few years you will have a house of your own. Large lots, high, dry and healthful. *All* suburban property near Boston must rapidly increase in value, as the city and its surroundings are steadily growing in population, and in the immediate future all towns and cities within a circle of 10 miles, will be a part of Boston and connected by Electric cars.

. . People who should buy lots on our easy payment plan: *Every man* with a family, who is not able to buy a home at once, but can spare a small sum each month. *The young man or young woman* who realizes that sometime they will want a home. A small sum each week will soon secure it, and you will hardly miss the money. *Every person* with a small sum to invest, who wants to be sure of a safe investment, and where there is every prospect of its doubling in value in a short time.

. . The largest fortunes in this country have been made by judicious investments in real estate. This is your chance. *Young married man*, as soon as you can, buy such a place, even if you have to put on it a mortgage reaching from base to cap-stone. *An easy payment mortgage the home buyer's friend.* The much abused mortgage, which is ruin to a reckless man, to one prudent and provident is the beginning of a competency and a fortune, for the reason that he will not be satisfied until he has paid it off, and all the household are put on stringent economies until then. *Deny yourself all superfluities and all luxuries until you can say: "Everything in this house is mine, every timber, every brick, every foot of plumbing, every door-sill."*

. . Winchester has the best of 12 R. R. accomodations. 85 trains a day. 31 Sundays. Fast trains. Only 15 minutes. Call or write for free tickets; good on any train. Also for list of daily excursions. No expense to see the land. Seeing is believing, believing is buying.

. . Winchester is unquestionably one of the most desirable residential towns in the vicinity of Boston, and until recently, no land has ever been offered at a price within the reach of ordinary people.

- TOWN HALL AND LIBARY -

. . Winchester Park is bounded on one side by the R. R. and on the other by Washington St., one of the principal and most beautiful avenues in the town, sixty feet wide and bordered on either side by large shade trees. The price at which these lots are placed upon the market, from $150 to $300, are less, we believe, than any equally desirable property has ever been offered, is within the reach of all, and will insure their immediate sale.

All we ask is that you look at this property before buying.

+ + + + + + + + + + + + +

53 State Street
Room 440

G. Marlon Keene

BOSTON

Agent

The North End was once home to a sizable black population, which came to Winchester from the declining agricultural South to work in its thriving industries. Many blacks lived on Irving and Harvard Streets, part of a racially balanced neighborhood called Winchester Park. The firemen aboard "Hose 3" served at the local Swanton Street fire station.

neighborhood until the late 1920s, when the black population began to decline and Italian immigrants bought up the houses.

The Richardson family owned almost all of the town land north of Cross Street and east of the Aberjona River. Four members of the family—Moses, James, Mathilda, and Roswell Richardson—owned the land between the river and Washington Street, which they called Aberjona Bend. In 1893 they divided this land into small house lots and planned streets called Clematis, Garfield, and Brookside, as well as an extension of Forest Street. They sold the lots to developers, who built houses for carpenters, machinists, a tannery foreman, and other employees of heavy industry in the North End. Today the area remains one of the most charming neighborhoods on the north side, with simple, vernacular variations of the Queen Anne and Shingle styles on winding, wooded streets.

On the other side of the river, squeezed between Cross Street and the Woburn line, were farms belonging to Eli Cooper and the brothers Samuel S. and Lemuel Holton. In 1872 Cooper sold his land to developers who planned to erect twenty houses west of Calvary Cemetery. The area proved to be too isolated, however, and only six houses went up over the next three decades, all on Baldwin Street. In 1874 the Holtons registered a plan to divide the back of their property into nine new streets with 231 house lots of 5,000 square feet each; the plan never got off the ground. In the 1870s the brothers managed to lay out only two streets, Holton and East, and build only two houses. By the end of the century developers built another eight houses on four additional streets—Verplast Avenue, Pine Grove Park, Highland View Avenue, and Adams Road—but the neighborhood had a confused, haphazard look.

The area south of Cross Street did not fare much better. In 1891 a development firm called the Suburban Land Improvement Company laid out a hundred house lots in the marshy area between Main Street and the Boston and Lowell Railroad tracks. The lots were small and affordable, averaging 2500 square feet and costing two hundred to four hundred dollars. The company's advertisements appealed to workers' aspirations to better their standard of living: "Own Your Own Home," the ads proclaimed, "You Can Do It." Unfortunately, the company was only partly successful. The region's marshes, fed by the nearby river and never fully drained, prevented the sale of many lots, and as a result the area has a random appearance with many dead ends.

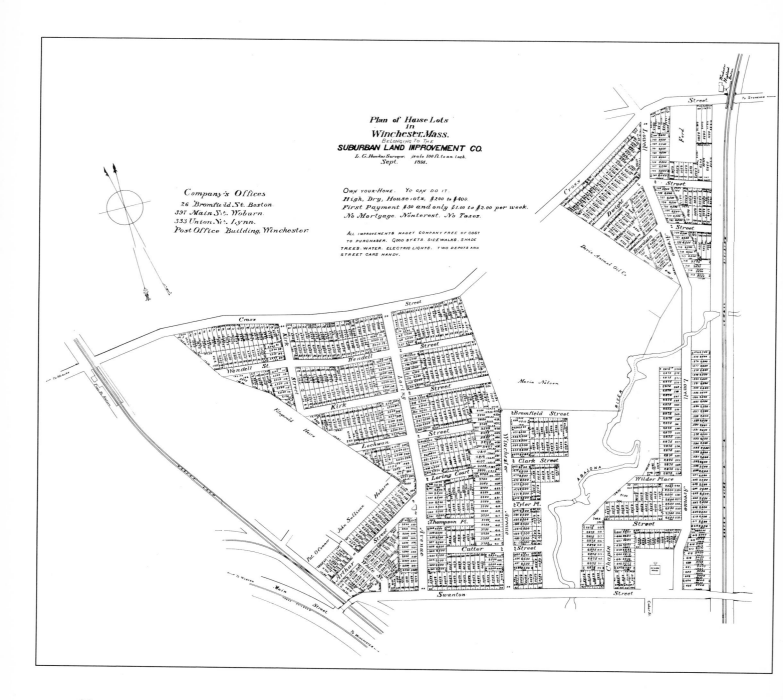

Plan of House Lots
in
Winchester, Mass.
BELONGING TO THE
SUBURBAN LAND IMPROVEMENT CO.
L. G. Hawkes Surveyor.   scale 100 ft. to an inch.
Sept.   1891.

Company's Offices
26 Bromfield St. Boston.
397 Main St. Woburn.
333 Union St. Lynn.
Post Office Building, Winchester.

OWN YOUR HOME.   YOU CAN DO IT.
High, Dry, House Lots, $200 to $400.
First Payment $30 and only $1.00 to $2.00 per week.
No Mortgage. No Interest. No Taxes.

ALL IMPROVEMENTS MADE BY COMPANY FREE OF COST
TO PURCHASER. GOOD STETS. SIDEWALKS. SHADE
TREES. WATER. ELECTRIC LIGHTS. TWO DEPOTS AND
STREET CARS HANDY.

Emergence of a True Victorian Town: Winchester Neighborhoods, 1830–1916

In 1891, The Suburban Land Improvement Company developed the marshy land between Main Street and the Boston & Lowell Railroad and encouraged workers to "own your own home."

A "Cutter Village" family home on Main Street, built in 1850 but no longer standing.

Still, there are about forty pre-1917 houses on the streets around Loring Field. These include six duplexes on Arthur Street that are nearly identical in style, and four well-preserved duplexes on Chapin Street and Chapin Court. The Irish and Italian immigrant workers who lived in this neighborhood at first rented houses from absentee landlords, then bought their own homes. These streets, though once overshadowed by the giant Puffer Manufacturing Company, managed to maintain an almost rural feeling through the years, and the untouched enclave of late-nineteenth-century worker housing still gives us a good idea of what the north side must have been like in Winchester's days of heavy industry.

West of Main Street, the patterns of development and ownership were similar to the rest of the North End. Several land-owning families, including the Cutters and the Churches, sold or developed their land when the town's population boomed in the 1880s and 1890s. Joshua Farrow, Benjamin Church, and others built small worker houses in a variety of styles on Canal, Richardson, Water, Salem, Farrow, and Clark Streets. Residents worked at the tanneries, the Eastern Felt Company, and Church and Lane Piano Manufacturers. Blank Brothers Tannery, situated where the town yard is now, was a big employer. John Blank bought up land west of the factory, laid out Middlesex Street, and built small, undistinguished tenant houses for his workers along the depression that was once the Middlesex Canal. Though the architecture is unexceptional, the street is a stylistically coherent example of late-nineteenth-century mass-produced worker housing.

There were a few upper-middle-class houses on Main Street, including several owned by the Cutter family, the industrialists Alexander Moseley and Stilman Nichols, and the George Russell family. But otherwise, the North End west of Washington Street was entirely working class, with an architectural heritage unlike any other part of Winchester.

East of Washington Street

East of Washington Street the complexion of the north side changed completely. Farther away from heavy industry than the Swanton neighborhood and situated on hilly terrain, this eastern slice of the North End did not lend itself to the neat development of worker houses. Here, builders saw an ideal location for larger, more expensive houses that would attract a more prosperous, middle-class resident. As a result, Washington Street became a sharp line of demarcation. With the exception of one small area, the houses east of the street had virtually no Irish or Italian owners until well into this century.

The exception was a little enclave of streets just north of the Center—Elm, Kendall, Stevens, and Bridge Streets. All four of these roads existed in 1854, and during the real estate boom that swept the Center after incorporation, many businessmen and property owners built here. Then, in the 1870s and 1880s, these streets became part of the flourishing Irish neighborhood centered around St. Mary's Church. For a long transitional period, this district had a unique residential mix, ranging from old Yankee families and wealthy businessmen to new Irish property owners and local artisans and tradesmen.

The Matten House at 6–8 Bridge Street is a good example of the pattern of ownership of the area. Samuel S. Richardson, the wealthy industrialist, property owner, and member of the old Winchester family, built the house before 1854; it is one of three houses he owned on Bridge and Kendall Streets. In 1865 he sold it to William Matten, a manufacturer of supplies to the shoe industry who came to Winchester at the end of the Civil War. Matten owned the house for nearly forty years, then sold it in 1904 to Alexander Mullen, a second-generation Irishman and member of the Winchester police force. Many houses in the neighborhood have a similar history and the streets always maintained a diverse population.

The houses here have little to distinguish them architecturally. Most are vernacular versions of the popular Greek Revival, Queen Anne, and Italianate styles. The Hawes-Webb House at 7 Stevens Street is a good example of the Mansard style, however, and the Gothic Revival Eustis House at 14 Stevens Street has acorn-drop gingerbread vergeboard that is unique in Winchester. Nearby, the Samuel B. White House at 8 Stevens has sinister, icicle-like vergeboard.

Washington Street, long dominated by the farms and shoe shops of the Richardson family, gradually attracted residents during the latter half

1

2

Residences in the North End were primarily vernacular examples of popular period styles (photo 1, 8 Stevens; photo 2, 67 Hemingway), many built for workers in the local mills. Washington Street, however, remained a fashionable place to live for many North End property owners, including the Richardsons (photo 3, 607 Washington).

3

of the nineteenth century. Some of Winchester's most prominent citizens, including the carpet merchant Jerome Judkins, the lawyer John T. Wilson, and Winchester's first tax collector, Samuel Kendall, built their homes here. Some wealthy North End property owners lived on Washington because it was fashionable yet close to their holdings. Joseph Guernsey and George and Caroline Payne, for example, lived on Washington Street and owned eight tenant houses between them on nearby Webster and Eaton Streets. The most architecturally impressive homes on Washington were Wilson's Mansard house at 179, now the Robert J. Costello Funeral Home, and Judkin's Italianate mansion at 162, now the residence of nuns associated with St. Mary's parish.

The streets running east off Washington, from Hancock Street in the south to Fairmont Street in the north, remained largely undeveloped until 1900. Judkins, who owned 35 acres east and north of his mansion, built four houses on Prince Avenue and Hancock Street before 1886, but for some reason building was very slow here compared to the way in which the Irish neighborhoods across the street had flourished. When construction did pick up between 1900 and 1910, the area filled in rapidly with houses in a variety of vernacular styles, larger than the worker houses across Washington Street. The original owners were middle class and Protestant—almost all of them had Yankee or Scandinavian names—and it was some time before Irish and Italians bought into the neighborhood.

But the most architecturally interesting section of the north side is along the Fells, the easternmost border of the town extending from Winthrop Street near the Center to Fells Road in the north. With houses close to both woods and main streets, this area bordering the Middlesex Fells Reservation is unlike any other part of Winchester—its atmosphere is more like that of a New Hampshire town. Most of the houses are vernacular Queen Anne buildings that out-of-town developers put up between 1886 and 1915. But the Fells also contains some of Winchester's most eclectic examples of architecture, especially on Highland Avenue and Hillcrest Parkway. In the early 1890s, when the Wedgemere Syndicate was active on the west side of town, Arthur T. Wyman planned a similar development on Highland Avenue. Unfortunately, the financial panic of 1893 had an even more devastating effect on Wyman's venture

Wedgemere developer Arthur Wyman also developed land along Highland Avenue near the Fells. He actively promoted Hillcrest on the basis of its natural beauty, but a down economy prevented the kind of building volume indicated in the plot plan.

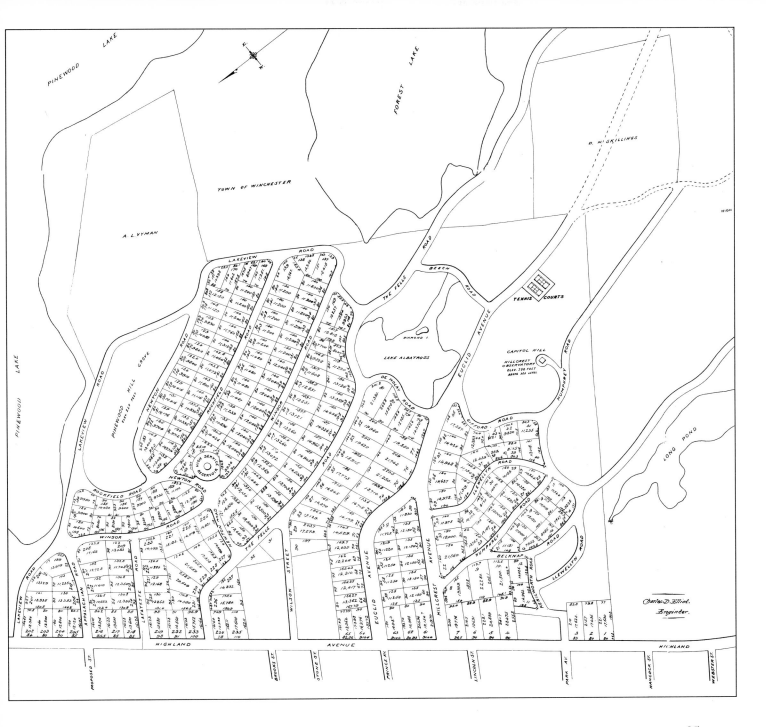

Out Washington Street: Immigrants and Industrialization

than it had on Wedgemere; very little building took place and Wyman lost a lot of money. But two houses from the development remain: the French House at 108 Highland Avenue and the Edward Braddock House at 112. Both houses are architecturally curious, but the Braddock House is a particularly interesting and successful mixture of Shingle and Colonial Revival styles. Braddock was an inventor who specialized in tinning and galvanizing and he held over a hundred patents. Coincidentally, another inventor, Edward Comfort, lived close by, in a Tudor house at 87 Highland Avenue.

Though nothing approaching the development of the Church Street area occurred in the Fells area, there was some construction after Wyman's unlucky experience, and soon the neighborhood was home to some of Winchester's leading businessmen and industrialists. But the Fells area was always remote, a thin slice of affluence at the edge of the predominantly working-class North End.

Chapter 4

Out Main Street: Individuality and Diversity

The physical landscape of the area south of the Center has a variety that no other section of Winchester can claim. From the Middlesex Fells to the Upper Mystic Lake, some of the town's most beautiful houses sit amidst forests, plains, hills, farmland, and lakeside lowlands. Penetrated by Main Street and encircled by two of the most scenic roads in Winchester, Mystic Valley Parkway and South Border Road, this area has a range of settings that makes it almost a smaller version of the town as a whole.

Historically, however, the section out Main Street differs from the rest of Winchester in two distinct ways. First, most of this area was originally part of the town of Medford. Black Horse Terrace, which today seems quite central, once marked the southernmost point of Woburn. Many of the residents who lived beyond that point felt socially and politically closer to Medford than to the budding village of South Woburn that later became Winchester. When South Woburn residents agi-

tated for incorporation in the 1840s, some of their Medford neighbors, including John and Marshall Symmes, signed a petition requesting that they not be included in the new town. This feeling of separateness persisted even after incorporation.

Second, one family, the Symmes, controlled much of the land. In 1618, when the town of Charlestown divided and allotted the wilderness of Woburn, Deacon Zachariah Symmes received 300 acres, by far the largest grant apportioned. Though the family later sold big portions of Zachariah's allotment to the Brooks and Bacon families, the old deacon's descendants continued to dominate the region until after 1900. For centuries the family was the biggest in Winchester, outnumbering even the Richardsons, and in no other section of the town did one family control so much property and commerce.

Yet in spite of these differences, the area out Main Street eventually showed tremendous social, economic, and architectural diversity. Like the geography, the man-made landscape had a variety that reflected the development of the entire town. The Symmes ran a large farm similar to the market farms west of Cambridge Street. The Bacon Felt Factory near the Upper Mystic Lake was the first large-scale industry in Winchester, and paralleled industrial development in both the Center and the North End. The area had the town's first commuter neighborhood and a number of Victorian developments like those west of the Center. The region also had a broad architectural range; worker houses, middle-class duplexes, and beautiful old mansions lined adjoining streets. By the end of the nineteenth century, the area out Main Street had become Winchester's most diversified district.

In the nineteenth century, three neighborhoods contained this diversity. From the intersection of Main and Washington Streets south to Herrick Street and east to Highland Avenue, an area once known as Black Horse Village was the first to develop. Farther south was Symmes Corner, the center of a very diverse neighborhood that developed more slowly as the Symmes family gradually sold sections of their farm. West of Symmes Corner, on land the Symmeses sold the Bacons in 1825, was Baconville, a unique enclave of family houses, factory buildings, and workers' houses that surrounded the Bacon Felt Company.

Black Horse Village

The intersection of Main and Washington Streets was the focal point of Winchester's first commuter neighborhood. From the 1830s on, many of the Boston businessmen who came to Winchester in the wake of the railroad built their homes on the streets of the old Black Horse Village. Directly south of the growing town center, this area was an ideal spot for the town's new residents. Together with members of Winchester's old families and some of the town's small industrialists, they created an elegant new neighborhood.

This part of town had always been an imposing location. Main Street, as the main road and stage route from Medford to Woburn and points north in the Merrimac Valley, attracted small industries, businesses, and stores throughout the eighteenth and early nineteenth centuries, and the famous Black Horse Tavern was one of the most popular rural inns in New England. But after the arrival of the railroad the area began to fill out with residences, and the growth of the Center gave

impetus to the development of a distinct neighborhood, stretching from the Center to the corner of Main and Herrick Streets.

Given its excellent location, the neighborhood soon became one of the finest in town. But growth was gradual. Between 1830 and 1916, there were two principal waves of development. The first occurred during the years of the town's early expansion and incorporation, from the coming of the railroad to the end of the Civil War. This period saw the transformation of the area from a country village to a town neighborhood. The roads running east from Washington and Main Streets grew from private paths to graded town ways, and the old farm pastures between Main Street and Highland Avenue gradually gave way to houses. The population of the neighborhood was an equal mixture of Winchester businessmen, old families, and Boston commuters, many of whom directed the government and social business of the town.

The second wave was more expansive but less significant. From the 1870s until after the turn of the century, the neighborhood filled up with attractive houses similar to those constructed in the area out Church

The intersection of Main and Washington Streets was once the site of the thriving Black Horse Village.

Street. Like other parts of town, the Black Horse Village neighborhood reflected the overall development of Winchester into a prosperous Victorian suburb. A much higher percentage of these new home owners were commuters, but unlike their first-wave counterparts, these Boston men tended to be less interested in town affairs. There were certainly exceptions—Forrest Manchester, who lived at 310 Main Street, was an obvious one—but like the town as a whole, this neighborhood lost some of its small town solidarity as it expanded.

Two old families, the Symmeses and the Johnsons, dominated this area during the 1830s and 1840s. Though the center of the Symmes's influence, Symmes Corner, was farther south on Main Street, the family was very extensive. In 1831, Horatio, Joseph, and Zachariah Symmes each owned a house in the neighborhood. Zachariah's property straddled the Medford-Woburn line; he was said to have his house in Woburn and his barn in Medford. None of their houses survives, but in 1854 Horatio Symmes built another house at 404 Main Street that still stands. In the same year Gardner Symmes, a local builder and town assessor, built the very attractive Italianate house at 417 Main Street. This house later became the property of Alfred Vinton, a Symmes in-law, lawyer, and author of the *Symmes Memorial,* a genealogy of the family. In 1834 Deacon John Symmes built a store and shoe shop across from his house at Symmes Corner that a later owner moved to 4 Fairview Terrace in 1892. Jefferson Ford, a famous ship captain and another Symmes in-law, lived in this house during the 1850s and 1860s.

But by this time the Johnsons had become the most important family in the neighborhood. They owned almost all the land now crossed by Mt. Pleasant Street, Crescent Road, and Hillside and Summit Avenues. They built at least seven houses in the neighborhood, including six clustered around the Johnson blacksmith shop at the intersection of Main and Washington Streets. Josephus Johnson, who helped in the construction of Wildwood Cemetery, lived nearby in a big late Federal house on Hillside Avenue. Later owners divided the house and moved its sections to 25 and 26 Crescent Road in 1893. All of the Johnsons took part in local business and politics, but the most influential member of the family by far was Nathan Johnson, deacon in the Congregational Church, one of the original town selectmen, and a leader in the fight for incorporation. His stern, tight-lipped, white-haired visage was a common sight at important events and meetings throughout the town's early history. In the 1850s Deacon Johnson laid out Mount Pleasant Street and Hillside Avenue. In 1855 he sold land to Clarimond Pierce, with the agreement that she maintain and grade the streets. Pierce built an Italianate house on the corner at 19 Mount Pleasant Street. Johnson also sold property on Summit Avenue to Emeline Bell, who built the Mansard house at number 6 in 1860. But the most beautiful house in the neighborhood was the one Nathan Johnson built for himself at 21 Washington Street. The Stanton House, as it is now known, is Winchester's finest example of the Greek Revival style. The house is named after the local businessman Jacob Stanton, who bought it in 1880 and moved it back from the road to its present position seven years later. The house is unusual in its succession of owners—no commuters have occupied it in its entire 145-year history—and it has been excellently maintained since its construction in 1840.

In 1904 Winchester completed a beautiful new high school (now the Lincoln Elementary School), the classical details of which reflected the educational ideals of the era. Today, the old back door serves as the main entry, originally on the Mystic Valley Parkway side and approached by way of an impressive, sweeping driveway.

Many other houses that went up during the first wave have a particularly high architectural value that is directly related to the town's early prosperity. The 1840s and 1850s were boom years for Massachusetts, and as related in the story of the Center, Winchester prospered as well as any industrial town in the state. The men who established industries near the Aberjona River and the new railroad often made substantial fortunes. Naturally they were eager to build homes that reflected their success, and these men joined the Boston lawyers and factory owners in the town's best neighborhoods. Appropriately, the two most popular architectural styles during this period, Greek Revival and Italianate, were lavish, detailed, and ornamental. These styles became associated with success. Nathan Johnson's handsome home was a symbol of his status in the town. The successful industrialist Harrison Parker built an attractive Italianate villa on Main Street in 1854; that house stands now at 60 Lloyd Street, where it was moved in 1898. Arthur Whitney, who started the Whitney Machine Company with his father, lived in a Greek Revival house at 354 Main Street. This house was also moved in the 1890s to 5 Mystic Avenue.

The Whitney House was probably the work of John H. Coates, the busiest builder in Winchester during the early years of the town. Enter-

Out Main Street: Individuality and Diversity

prising and reliable, Coates built at least a dozen houses along Main Street. He also built extensively beyond Symmes Corner, between Grove Street and the railroad tracks, where he had bought six acres from John Symmes in 1850. His work spanned at least three decades: around 1843 he built the Hatch House, which now stands at 26 Grove Street; thirty years later he built the Tyler House at 7 Herrick Street.

All of Coates's houses were either Greek Revival or Italianate. He built for local people (such as the town druggist Joseph Hovey), relatives, and commuters. Later owners often altered Coates's designs, but fortunately they did so tastefully and this neighborhood, like most in Winchester, retained its architectural integrity. We can get a good idea of this integrity from three adjacent Coates houses on the west side of Main Street: 326, 336, and 346. All of these houses occupy generous lots in one of the nicest parts of the neighborhood. The Grafton House at 326 is an unaltered Greek Revival, but the others see a combination of Coates's original design and later alteration. All the houses are beautiful, and while Coates must be given his due, later owners deserve much credit for keeping the styles handsome and unified.

Two of early Winchester's most interesting residents built their homes on the fringe of the Main and Washington Street neighborhood. Lutherina Teele, a town activist and early feminist, built a house at the corner of Winthrop Street and Highland Avenue. Teele was a prominent member of the Women's Christian Temperance Movement and the Women's Suffrage League. Ahead of her time in many respects, she willed the house to two women, close friends of hers.

The artist and naturalist Edward Brackett lived at 220 Highland Avenue. Brackett bred pheasants in the Fells behind his house and built a fish hatchery on South Border Road; he later served for a long time on the Winchester Fish Commission. During the Civil War Brackett was active in the Underground Railway. Brackett was a poor man, and when he built his house in 1856 he combined his need for economy with his artist's sensibility and his love of nature by choosing an octagon style. He based his building on designs from a book by another nineteenth-century eccentric, Orson Fowler, who argued that the octagon shape was the most economical for construction, and also provided maximum light and ventilation. The house required no frame, but rather a lattice crib of

The octagon house of artist Edward Brackett at 220 Highland, now stuccoed over but otherwise retaining its unique period style.

Emergence of a True Victorian Town: Winchester Neighborhoods, 1830–1916

boards. Four separate octagons, varied in height, constitute Brackett's house, which still stands sturdily among the trees of the Middlesex Fells. The original wooden facade is now stuccoed over, but the characteristic style shines through.

Most of the residents who arrived in the neighborhood during the second wave of development were more conventional than Brackett or Teele, however. In 1861, eighty-nine Winchester citizens had businesses in Boston, and many chose the convenient Black Horse Village area for their homes. Businessmen like Moses Herrick, the coffee merchant James Dwinell, and Preston Pond bought up property here and built large houses for themselves. Herrick lived on Highland Avenue, near the corner of the street that now bears his name. Dwinell lived in a Coates house on Main Street, and Pond owned an estate on which he built a string of properties on Prospect Street, the center of which was his Queen Anne–style house at number 8. In the 1870s, John C. Mason bought up much of the land on Hillside Avenue and Crescent Street, and in 1893 he divided most of his land into house lots that he sold for development. Gradually the neighborhood came to resemble the way it looks today.

The houses that appeared during the second wave show a greater variety of styles than the first: Queen Anne, Tudor, Shingle Style, Colonial Revival, and Mansard. These Late Victorian styles were popular throughout America during the last quarter of the nineteenth century. They indicate the era's prosperity, eccentricity, and interest in the past. The Russell House at 10 Mount Pleasant Street is one of Winchester's best examples of the Tudor style. Number 387 Main Street is a fascinating example of Colonial Revival with a distinctive projecting central gable. Several Shingle-style houses, including some ambitious examples are at 6, 7, 14, and 16 Prospect Street. A man named William Belcher, a manufacturer of an early version of the typewriter that he called a "Caligraph Writing Machine," lived in the latter. In 1892 Preston Pond tore down the Black Horse Tavern and opened up Black Horse Terrace for development. Robert Coit, the architect who designed the public library and the houses of the Firth Development, designed the Shingle style/Queen Anne house at 6 Black Horse Terrace for the Boston broker Arthur Hale. Coit also helped the prominent local artist Herman Dudley

Robert Coit, architect of the public library and the Firth Development, built this house at 6 Black Horse Terrace after Preston Pond opened up the street for development.

Murphy design a studio next to Murphy's Tudor villa at 314–316 Highland Avenue; three of Murphy's paintings now reside in the Boston Museum of Fine Arts. Coit himself lived at 19 Hillside Avenue. Most of the new residents who arrived in the 1880s and 1890s, the neighborhood's greatest period of growth, had little interest in town affairs. Winchester was no longer a small town.

The area around Symmes Corner, "remote" from the town center, remained rural well into the mid-1800s.

Symmes Corner

Unlike the Black Horse Village neighborhood, the area surrounding Symmes Corner remained rural, scattered, and dominated by a single family until well after incorporation. There were several reasons for this difference. Because the neighborhood was over half a mile from the town center, it was a less attractive site for commuter residences. There was also a definite feeling of separateness to the area, primarily because this region was part of Medford until 1850. But the biggest reason was the presence of the Symmes family itself. By far the largest in Winchester, the family built more houses and owned more land than any other family in the town. Even though sales of large lots had whittled down Zachariah Symmes's original seventeenth-century grant considerably, in 1850 the family still owned most of the southern end of town. The first map of Winchester, published in 1854, illustrated how dominant the family was at the time: fourteen of the twenty-two houses and shops south of Mystic Avenue and east of the Bacon Estate belonged to the Symmeses. John and Marshall Symmes owned houses and businesses at Symmes Corner. Radiating out from the corner, like spokes from the hub of a wheel, were the various residences, small industries, businesses, and farmhouses of the family. Gardner Symmes, who ran a sash and blind shop in Samuel S. Richardson's mill complex, was the area's biggest builder. Horatio Symmes owned a general store on Main Street. The family owned blacksmith shops, wheelwright shops, and shoe shops. It built bridges and laid roads. In 1850, Marshall Symmes laid out Mystic Avenue, the only side street in the neighborhood that existed before 1860, and built three houses—20, 30, and 34–36. The family also owned and ran a large farm that was still in operation after 1900.

Emergence of a True Victorian Town: Winchester Neighborhoods, 1830–1916

Many of the Symmes's neighbors were men who married into the family and settled near Symmes Corner. Hosea Dunbar, one of the founders of the Winchester Unitarian Society, married Deacon John Symmes's daughter and built the Greek Revival house at 11 Grove Street on land he bought from his father-in-law in 1853. Marshall Symmes's daughter Ella married the market gardener James Russell, one of the largest celery growers in Massachusetts and a charter member of the Boston Market Gardeners Association; they lived in the Mansard house at 86 Main Street. Oliver Wellington, another Symmes in-law, built a Greek Revival house at 15 Chestnut Street in 1861.

But the Symmeses weren't the only residents in the neighborhood; there were also a few early commuters and local businessmen. John Coates built two houses on the Grove Street acreage that John Symmes sold him in 1850—one for himself at 19 and one at 15 for the lawyer and editor Edwin Wadleigh. Mariner Isaac Knapp and piano maker Sylvanus Elliot lived on Chestnut Street, which opened up in the 1860s. J. H. Prince built two houses on Madison Avenue in the late 1860s, and William Redfern, a member of a large lumber-dealing family, lived on Oak Knoll, where the Parkhurst House now stands. Albert Ayer moved the Redfern House to 11 Sanborn Street in 1893. Ayer and his brother Thomas were prominent businessmen who moved to Winchester in the 1860s. Both were selectmen, and Thomas was a member of almost every important town committee for decades. He lived in an Italianate house at 8 Grove Street and Albert at a similar house at 8 Brooks Street.

After the Civil War, when the town expanded and large industry arrived in Winchester, more people became interested in the Symmes Corner neighborhood as a residential area. In the late 1860s, about the time that David N. Skillings developed Rangeley on the west side of the Center, Abijah and Stephen Thompson planned a similar estate along the Aberjona River at the foot of Mystic Avenue. The Thompsons ran the tannery their father had established on Manchester Field, and wanted to take advantage of the land they owned just south of the factory. The location was promising—the land was level and the view excellent. But after grading and filling the land, the brothers abandoned the project. Ironically, they felt the site was too close to the industrial landscape that included their own tannery.

As Winchester industry developed, many people associated with the new factories moved to the area out Main Street. One of Winchester's most famous residents, the inventor Louis Goddu, established an enclave of houses in the Symmes Corner neighborhood where he, his wife, and thirteen children lived for decades. Goddu worked for the McKay Metallic Fastener Company in the 1860s and 1870s, and later ran his own business out of his carriage house. He was a prolific inventor; when he died, he owned over 300 patents, most of them in the important field of shoe machinery. Goddu is best known, however, for his invention of the simple wire staple.

In 1865 Goddu built a Mansard house at 13 Madison Avenue, but most of the family's houses went up in the 1890s, when Goddu's children came of age and built Queen Anne houses on Madison Avenue, Chestnut Street, and Goddu Avenue. The Goddu estate lay on hills overlooking the southern end of Winchester. At the time, the estate was isolated; the area has since filled in, but the Goddu houses remain an unusual family enclave.

Throughout the 1880s, 1890s, and the first decade of the twentieth century, the Symmes family continued to build, erecting family homes and tenant houses on Main Street, Madison Avenue, and Sanborn Street. The family opened up Symmes Road and Madison Avenue West and sold lots to builders. But these were also years of expansion for the town, and many commuters spilled over from the central neighborhoods. During the 1890s, Chestnut Street and Grove Street filled out. Lawson Street opened up at the turn of the century, named after Thomas Lawson, the financier and copper magnate who lived at 336 Main Street. In 1893 Lewis Parkhurst bought Oak Knoll from the Symmes family and built his isolated, ornamental, and picturesque mansion that still looks grandly down upon the town. Also during the 1890s, many worker houses went up on Cutting Street and Mystic Avenue, homes for employees of the Cutting Lumber Yard on Manchester Field.

After 1900, suburban developments began to change the face of the Symmes Corner neighborhood. Three distinct developments appeared between the turn of the century and 1916. In 1902, Charles Ogden bought up Symmes land directly south of Symmes Corner and laid out Park, Ridgefield, Edgehill, and Bruce Roads. Over the next decade he built 32 houses here in a variety of styles. Farther north, on Lloyd and Maxwell Streets, Frank Ferguson built 33 houses around the same time. Like the houses of the Firth Development west of the Center, Ferguson's houses sat close together and appealed to middle-class renters and buyers, but each house is unique. Then in 1913, Eustace Brigham built five varied houses between Mystic Avenue and Lloyd Street on Mystic Valley Parkway. The houses overlook the fields bordering the Aberjona River, a pleasant spot that ironically adjoins the area that the Thompson brothers concluded was such a bad location.

Baconville

Until the early nineteenth century, the Symmes family owned all the land between Mystic Valley Parkway and Everett Avenue. The Upper Mystic Lake now covers that land, but before 1863 a large salt meadow, traversed by the meandering Aberjona River, spread west of Symmes Corner. Though marshy and unsuited to building, the meadow was a valuable haying field and source of bog iron for the family's farm and forge. The river provided power for two mills that served the family for over a century. But in 1824 the Symmeses sold the meadow and their mill privileges to Robert Bacon. From then on the Bacon family dominated this section, which became known as Baconville.

Bacon came to Winchester from Boston, where he had apprenticed in the felt-making trade. He learned his business well and, utilizing his control of recent patents on improvements in felting machinery, established a felt factory on one of the old Symmes mill sites. Successful from the start, Bacon soon ran a factory complex of ten buildings on and around an island in the river. The Bacon factory was the first large-scale industry in Winchester and the only such enterprise to antedate the coming of the railroad. When the railroad did arrive, the family discovered they had unwittingly found the perfect spot for the factory, which profited greatly from its proximity to the new railway line.

The Bacon business was very much a family one, and in 1833 Robert's son John established himself in the trade. Like his father, John invented some valuable machinery improvements and built his own mill.

Another son, Thomas, ran a hat store in Boston that the family business supplied. The family also leased factory space to local businessmen. During the boom years of the 1840s and 1850s a number of small industries operated out of the Bacon mills, including a cotton batting factory, a sash and blind shop, and a mahogany sawmill. By 1861, the year of Robert Bacon's death, the family was probably the most financially successful in Winchester.

Fortunately, the family moved the business upriver long before the city of Charlestown, in need of additional water during the Civil War, received authority from the Massachusetts legislature to erect a dam between the Upper and Lower Mystic Lakes. The dam raised the level of the old Upper Lake by six feet and flooded the sites of the old Symmes mills, which the city had taken by eminent domain. Symmes meadow, which John Bacon had cultivated well enough to gain widespread admiration for his gardens, also went underwater, and though Bacon successfully sued the Charlestown Water Commission, he probably didn't bother to collect the small settlement the court awarded him.

The Bacons were a dominant presence in the area for over a century. Though the factory is now gone, and the river rerouted, the business survived until 1951 in spite of a series of natural disasters that afflicted the mills and factories. Throughout the 135 years of its operation, the industry was a large employer with an especially big concentration of Irish employees, many of whom lived in a worker housing complex at Grove Place. Unlike many Winchester industrialists, the Bacons always lived close to their factories and workers; as a result, the area has an architectural variety and social integrity that few Winchester neighborhoods can claim.

When Robert Bacon first moved to Winchester he lived in an old Symmes house beside his new mill, but by 1830 he had done well enough to build himself the most impressive house in the neighborhood and one of the most impressive houses in the whole town, at 6 Mystic Valley Parkway. A handsome house with brick ends and a double chimney, Bacon's mansion stands close to the point where the Aberjona River empties into the Upper Mystic Lake and greets cars entering Winchester via the parkway. The year 1830 is the dividing line in American archi-

The home of Robert Bacon at 6 Mystic Valley Parkway. The Bacon family owned a successful felt manufacturing business in Winchester for nearly 130 years.

tecture between the Federal and Greek Revival styles, and the Bacon House is an excellent example of the transition, displaying distinctive characteristics of both styles. The existence of the original architect's design, the carpenter's bill, and the plasterer's contract increase the importance of this house, which is a potential nominee in the National Register of Historic Places.

John Bacon moved into his father's old house in 1830, but a few years later he too moved across the river, where he built a house for himself on the rising ground that is now Lakeview Road. From there he ran the family business, cultivated his gardens, traveled to the Far East, and oversaw the hundred acres of land the family owned between the railroad tracks and Church Street. He retired in 1882 and handed over control of the firm to his son Charles, who lived on Grove Street. By this time the area was known as Baconville, a name that included not only the Bacon family houses, but also tenant houses, the factory complex, and the worker housing on Grove Place. This distinct enclave is a microcosm of the town as a whole, and reminds us not only of the Bacons' influence, but also of the social, economic, and architectural variety of the town of Winchester.

Part III

Neighborhood Walking Tours and Architectural Survey

Part Three comprises five architectural walking tours that provide a panorama of Winchester's architectural heritage and bring the history of Winchester's architectural development to life. Paralleling the text in Parts One and Two, the tours span two hundred years not only of a town's development, but also of changing architectural tastes and styles. The major styles represented in these tours are illustrated on the following pages; to get the greatest enjoyment from the tours, we suggest that you review these illustrations before you go. In particular, note how differences in the design of windows, doors, rooflines, siding, and other basic features of a house can dramatically alter its character. Soon you will be able to identify a building's architectural style on your own by looking at these elements.

Each house tour begins with a map of the area; an inset outline of the town with the tour area shaded serves as a quick point of reference. Following each map are photos and descriptions of the houses or buildings on the tour, keyed by number to corresponding numbers on the maps. Most of the information on these houses and buildings was documented in a comprehensive survey of Winchester's architecture conducted by the Winchester Historical Commission between 1976 and 1979. As you will see, Winchester possesses a wealth of beautiful, interesting, and historic buildings that deserve not only appreciation, but also preservation.

Federal
1780–1830

prominent chimneys

gable roof

6/6 sash windows

brick sides

portico

fanlight

sidelights

columns

Greek Revival
1830–1860

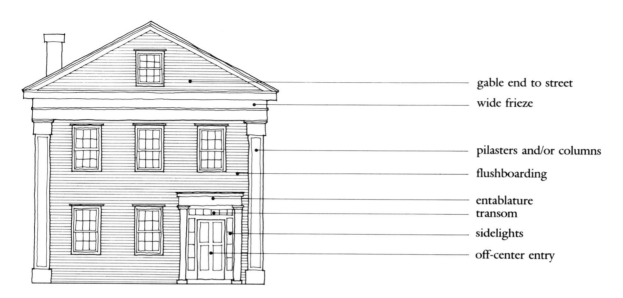

gable end to street

wide frieze

pilasters and/or columns

flushboarding

entablature

transom

sidelights

off-center entry

Gothic Revival
1835—1875

steeply pitched roof
with cross-gable

decorative vergeboards

pointed arched windows

vertical siding

porch with
flattened pointed arches

Italianate
1845–1880

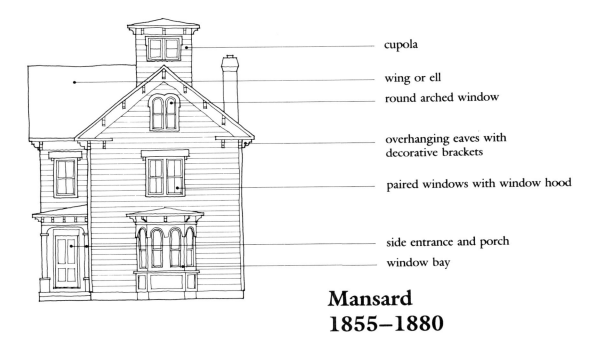

cupola

wing or ell

round arched window

overhanging eaves with
decorative brackets

paired windows with window hood

side entrance and porch

window bay

Mansard
1855–1880

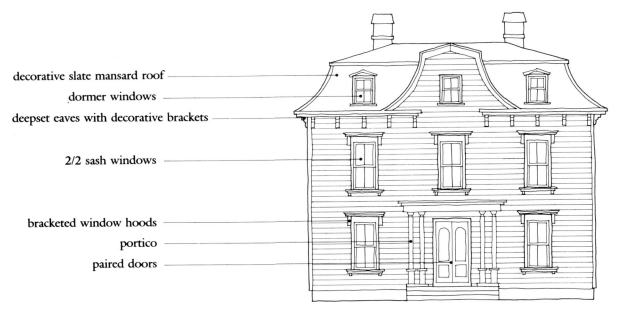

decorative slate mansard roof

dormer windows

deepset eaves with decorative brackets

2/2 sash windows

bracketed window hoods

portico

paired doors

Queen Anne
1875–1910

tall decorative chimneys

mixed siding
multipaned windows

bay windows

turret or tower

large porch
spindlework at porch balustrades

Shingle
1880–1900

eyebrow window

recessed window

banded windows
wood shingles
multilevel eaves
covered porch

heavy porch supports

Colonial Revival
1885–1910

roof dormers

dentils under eaves

palladian window

pairs of multipaned
double-hung windows

balustered porch over entry

symmetrical facade

sidelights at entry

columned entry porch

Tudor
1890–1940

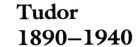

steeply pitched roof

dominant cross-gable

massive decorated chimney

decorative half-timbering

stucco wall cladding

brick lower story

tall, narrow multipane
casement windows

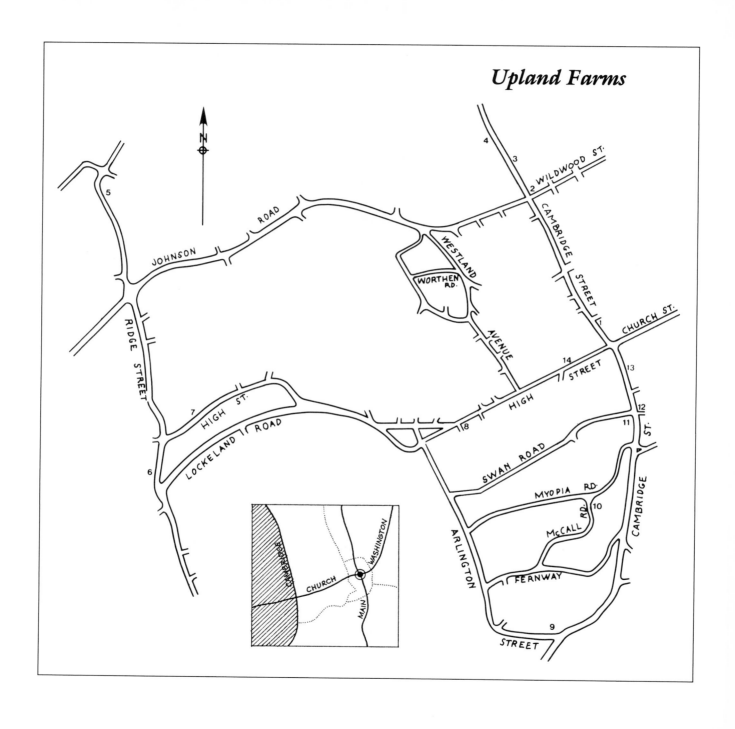

Upland Farms

117 Cambridge Street
c. 1775?/c. 1836

Parts of this house may date back to 1775 but it was rebuilt after 1836 by Loring Emerson, a founder of Winchester and one of its first selectmen. A Mansard roof was added later and then removed in the 1960s along with some trim. However, the Mansard style is still reflected in the four-bay facade, in the central dormer window with flanking pilasters, and in a remaining portion of Mansard roof on the back ell with its pedimented windows. A fan window above the front entrance mirrors the half-round window in the oak door.

(1)

93 Wildwood Street
c. 1843

Samuel W. Twombly, a Boston florist, came to Winchester in the 1850s. His home is a vernacular Greek Revival-style house with two-story Doric columns that draw attention to the side portico with its extended gable and windowed pediment. The columns at the front entryway are turned spindles. Twombly became active in town affairs and served as selectman, assessor, and on the committee to consider the building of a town hall. He was president of the Village Improvement Association in 1884 and was instrumental in acquiring town land for a common. He was also one of the developers of the land along Wildwood, Harrison, and Lawrence Streets.

(2)

195 Cambridge Street
c. 1826–1831

This house may stand on the site of one of the earliest homes in this area, which was built in 1660 by Richard Gardner and later owned by Hezekiah Wyman, the "White Horseman" famous for fighting the British in Arlington on April 19, 1775. The present house was built between 1826 and 1831 by George Wyman, farmer and rope spinner. The architecture is typical of the farmhouses on Cambridge Street, with a Greek Revival entrance with sidelights topped with a pointed arch and surrounded by decorative molding. Inside are wide pine floorboards, a delicate circular staircase, and finely crafted woodwork.

(3)

228 Cambridge Street
c. 1831

This was one of three houses—including no. 232, converted from a squash house in 1935, and no. 236, a foreman's house—built by Luke Reed around 1831. It was known after 1879 as the "Russel Farm," and was famous in the Boston market for fine garden produce. In 1947 the farm was sold to the Mahoney family, who developed it into the well-known nursery, "Mahoney's Rocky Ledge."

(4)

201 Ridge Street
1711

Built in 1711 by Josiah Johnson, a housewright, this is the oldest house in Winchester. It has been owned by one family, the Johnson-Thompsons for 275 years. Originally a transitional First Period house with two-over-two windows and a central chimney, it now has a central stairway, two chimneys, and a kitchen ell added in 1837. When clapboards were replaced with shingles in the 1970s 3" × 4" red oak studs and mortise and tenon joints on the cornerposts were exposed; and the removal of roof shingles revealed 22"-wide shingles covered with bark. Across the street at 202 Ridge stands a house built in 1820 by the brother of one of the owners of this house. Both were wheelwrights and maintained the farm in partnership.

(5)

78 Ridge Street
1828

On land previously farmed by Philemon Wright, an early settler of Winchester and the founder of Ottawa, and using part of his house's foundation, Asa Locke built this Federal-style clapboard farmhouse in 1828. Later changes included the addition of dormers and the removal of the wings of the house around 1910, one of which became the house at 114 Johnson Road. Also added later was the Greek Revival trim as seen in the classical porch pillars, the pediment, and the sidelight windows at the doorway. An 80' × 30' barn bears the date of 1827, and other farm buildings also survive. After 174 years in the Locke family, the farm was sold to the Hamiltons, who still maintain a working farm here.

(6)

195 High Street
c. 1803

This Federal-style house was built by Captain Josiah Locke, brother of Asa, who built 78 Ridge Street. When Captain Locke drowned in 1818, the house was divided in ownership among his heirs for many years thereafter. In 1911 it was acquired by the father of Maribel Vinson Owen; she and her daughters were world-class figure skaters until they were killed in an airplane accident in 1961. The front and most of the rear facades retain their original clapboards. The west ell, damaged by fire in about 1940, was rebuilt to its original appearance; the east ell was added in the mid-nineteenth century and retains much of the early construction. The side of the house most exposed to view has a fancy Flemish-bond brick pattern, while the other has a common bond.

(7)

68 High Street
1857

This house was built in 1857 by Asa Locke, a well-known market gardener, and occupied by his son Elbridge. It shows both Greek Revival and Italianate influences in the pedimented roof, pilasters, and Italianate porch. Noteworthy are the round-headed windows and the door with a transom over it. A series of ells were extended from the main house by later owners, one of whom was Handel Pond of the Ivers and Pond Piano Company, who acquired the house in 1902.

(8)

1 Arlington Street
1914

Jere Downes, a banker and donor of the Unitarian Church bells, built this Tudor-style house in 1914. The simulated half-timbering with stucco infill on the second story; the patterned brickwork beneath it; and the multipaned grouped windows copy the architectural details of Tudor houses in 16th-century England. Also common to this style are the numerous tall chimneys, the cross-gables, and the asymmetrical plan.

(9)

4 McCall Road
1904

This impressive house was occupied for many years by one of the most prominent citizens of Winchester, Samuel McCall, a member of Congress for twenty years and then Governor of Massachusetts for three terms ending in 1919. The house is in the Tudor style, with deep eaves, grouped windows with small lights, an overhanging second story, and massive chimneys. Landscaping was done by the world-famous firm of Frederick Law Olmstead.

(10)

4 Swan Road
1909

Built in 1909 by Joseph Remick in a neoclassical style derived from the Chicago Fair of 1893, this house was popularly known as the "Baby Sanborn" because of its resemblance to the more elaborate house built at 15 High Street two years earlier. Interestingly, it was acquired in 1947 by a son of the family who had lived in the Sanborn House. Although Remick's house has a balustrade and dentil detail similar to that of the Sanborn House, its windows are quite distinct: three pedimented windows with ornate molding contrast with the plainer, elongated windows beside and above them. There is also a wide decorative frieze beneath the cornice.

(11)

89 Cambridge Street
c. 1740–1750

The earliest part of this Colonial house was probably built between 1740 and 1750. It has a two-over-two plan and a large center chimney resting on a square base of fieldstone; the roof slants to a saltbox shape in the rear. After 100 years of ownership by the Swan family, the house was acquired by F. Patterson Smith, a Colonial Revivalist architect, who renovated it extensively in the 1930s. A shoe-shop wing and the west ell were removed and made into the house at 7 Gardner Place, and the barn was converted into 2 Gardner Place.

(12)

103 Cambridge Street
after 1825

This vernacular Federal-style house was probably built after 1825 for Patience and Sarah Gardner, sisters who lived here until 1864. Erroneously known as the "1776 House." it was said to have been built on the foundation of a much earlier house owned by Richard Gardner, one of the first settlers and ancestor of the Gardner sisters. The low foundation is of stone with brick facing and is only under half the house. The front of the house is clapboarded, the rear shingled. The barn has diagonal wood slat doors and interesting diamond-shaped windows.

(13)

15 High Street
1908

The "Sanborn House" was built in 1908 by Oren Cheney Sanborn, son of one of the founders of the Chase and Sanborn Company, at a reputed cost of $250,000. This stucco mansion, of the Beaux Arts Classical Revival style, is dominated by two-story columns with stacked Corinthian and Ionic capitals and a typical roof-top balustrade with dentil moldings. A drawing room and parlor led to a summer porch on one side; on the other was a kitchen and servants' quarters. Inside, ceilings are elaborately molded in a classical pattern and there is much oak and mahogany paneling. The arched window over the door incorporates multiple layers of glass of various tints and textures. The Downes family acquired the property in 1921; and in 1947 they sold it for use as a school to the Roman Catholic Church, who later sold it to the town.

(14)

Upland Farms

Winchester Center

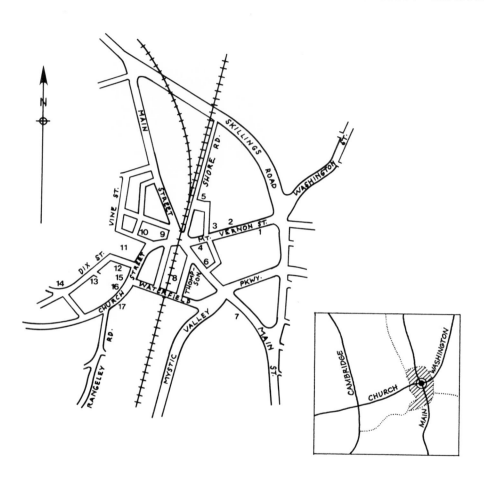

71 Mt. Vernon Street
1887

The headquarters of town government overlooks the mill pond that provided water power to a 17th-century grist mill. Boston architects Rand and Taylor designed the massive, asymmetrical building after the style of Henry Hobson Richardson's Romanesque architecture. This is especially evident in the east wing, which is one mass of granite and stone with arched windows similar to those of the Harvard Law School designed by Richardson in 1881. Other Romanesque features are the massive tower, the arched cave-like entryway to the auditorium, the arcade front, the arched windows, and the interlocking geometric layout. The windows are grouped in twos, threes, and fours and include two eyebrow windows on the roof. The building is constructed of red brick trimmed with Longmeadow freestone and has a foundation of Rockport granite and a roof of slate with copper flashing.

(1)

36 Mt. Vernon Street
1914

This neoclassical–style fire station was designed by Edward R. Wait for the Fire Department's new motorized equipment. It was the third fire house; the first was built on the site of the Winchester Cooperative Bank in 1857, and the second on Winchester Place in 1873. The two-story building is constructed of red brick in Flemish bond with cast-stone trim. It has monumental, stylized Corinthian pilasters, a cornice with dentil molding, a round porthole-style window in the gable, classical window caps, and a cupola based upon 18th-century design for public buildings. The three-bay facade has rusticated stonework outlining each bay.

(2)

26 Mt. Vernon Street
1892

The former Winchester Savings Bank building reflects the influence of the great American architect Henry Hobson Richardson. It is Romanesque in style and was designed and built by Edwin K. and William E. Blaikie, who were active in Winchester's development during the late nineteenth century. The asymmetrical massing of the building displays a gabled front with a Palladian window in the second floor. The paneled brick chimney and conical-roofed tower with fish-scale slate roof display features of the Queen Anne period, as do the modillions under the cornice and the dentils beneath them. The windows in the tower are topped by arched molding. Different colors and textures of brick and stone are used on this building, a common Richardsonian feature. The brick is laid in Flemish bond with Lake Superior sandstone seen in the entry and window surrounds. The entrance is strictly Richardsonian in its arched cave-like design flanked by short, grouped Romanesque columns of Tennessee marble with leafy cushioned capitals.

(3)

5–13 Mt. Vernon Street
1870

This late 19th-century business building known as the White Block contains neo-classical decoration in the brickwork. Samuel B. White, a Boston businessman, local builder, and property owner, was the original owner. A dry-goods store was there by 1893, and in 1915 it housed a popular ice-cream-and-candy store. An active YMCA occupied the building from 1890 to 1905, and it was commonly referred to by that name.

(4)

43 Shore Road
c. 1835

This vernacular Greek Revival–style home set back from the street and nearly hidden from view by other buildings has a late-Federal-style layout with its five-across symmetrical facade. Below the roofline is an entablature, and the corners are decorated with pilasters. The entry-way has fluted Doric columns, and the gable ends of the house are pedimented.

(5)

553–589 Main Street
1879

The Brown and Stanton building is an excellent example of a panel-brick Queen Anne business block. To appreciate and observe the features of the building, one must look above the changes made on the first floor facade during the 1950s. The slate hip roof is steep and intersected by gables that have large, arched windows made up of smaller panes. At the corner of Mt. Vernon Street is a tower with a conical roof. The vergeboards are solidly decorated with multicolored, patterned brickwork, and the facade displays trim of pressed red brick with burnt headers and elaborate corbeling. The building originally housed the community's post office, savings bank, town offices, and public library.

(6)

476 Main Street
1899

The Italianate home of Harrison Parker was moved from this site to 60 Lloyd Street when the Unitarian Society decided to build a new church to replace the one that was destroyed by fire; that one had stood further along Main Street, beyond the present McCall Junior High School. The architects of the present church were Perry, Dean, Hepburn, and Stewart Walker. The church is English Gothic Revival style with a square tower, buttressing, arched doorways, and windows, the latter with beautiful tracery. The church contains a large stained-glass window that commemorates the founding of the American Red Cross.

(7)

33–35 Thompson Street
1846

This Greek Revival–style house, built four years before the town separated from South Woburn, was the home of the first physician in South Woburn, Dr. William Ingalls. It is representative of several mid-to-late-19th-century houses in the Center that were later converted to commercial use. It has a pedimented front with a pair of quarter-round windows and an entablature below the roofline. Corner boards, instead of pilasters, decorate the building's edges, and there is a recessed entryway, typical of vernacular houses of this style. The first-floor bay window is a modern alteration.

(8)

568–572 Main Street
c. 1889

Samuel B. White, for whom this building is named, was in the leather business in Boston, where he was also a builder and owner of real estate. In the 1890s a drugstore and Sanderson's Hardware were occupants on the ground floor, while a dentist and telephone exchange were located on the second floor. The third floor had a hall for parties and a dancing school. In 1951 this structure suffered a fire and the top floor was removed and the remaining building remodeled. A close look at the second floor shows some of the original decorative brickwork.

(9)

1 Elmwood Avenue
1843

Originally a school at the corner of
Church and Dix Streets, this building
was moved to its present site in 1865
and converted to a two-family residence.
In 1928 Kelley and Hawes, who had an
express company and embalming establishment on Shore Road, converted it to
a funeral home; in 1985 it was acquired
by the Winchester Cooperative Bank. A
brick Colonial Revival facade and detailing cover the original wood clapboard.

(10)

21 Church Street
1854

Closely connected with the founding of
the community, the First Congregational
Church grew out of the desire of residents of South Woburn to have a meetinghouse of their own. Their decade-long
struggle led not only to the new church,
but to a new town as well. The first
structure on this site burned in 1853,
and the present building was dedicated
one year later. It was remodeled in 1884
and again in 1926 by the architect Robert Coit. The church has Italianate and
Romanesque features as seen in the projecting central steeple tower, elongated
arched windows, bracketed cornice, and
arched-front entryway. In 1926 the parish house at the western end was rebuilt
in the half-timbered Tudor style.

(11)

4 Dix Street
1912

This Tudor-style house was owned by
Daniel Kelley, co-founder of Kelley and
Hawes Livery, which was located in a
gambrel-roofed barn (1896) at 19–23
Shore Road, now a warehouse. Kelley
also operated undertaking, embalming,
storage, and express services. The home
is of stucco with half-timbering and has a
steep roof marked by multiple gables. A
deep overhang at the roofline sets off
walls with grouped, paired, and bay windows.

(12)

12 Dix Street
1900

This Colonial Revival two-and-one-half-story home has a hip roof with a very deep overhang, a porch with paired columns, and a balustrade. There is a large entryway, a three-sided bay, a rounded bay, and a second-floor Palladian window.

(13)

19 Dix Street
1854

The design of this house was probably taken from an A. J. Downing pattern book of English country houses. It has a jerkin roofline reminiscent of a straw-thatched Medieval English cottage. The front gable has stick work, and there are numerous sharp gables, a bay, and paired windows on this unusual home.

(14)

31 Church Street
1902

Designed by architect Allan E. Boone, this brick apartment building's original tenants were all physicians. This part of Church Street became known as "Doctors' Row" around the turn of the century, when many of the single-family homes also housed doctors and their practice. (Houses at 27, 40, and 45 Church are examples.) This three-story building shows a mixture of architectural styles popular at the turn of the century. The front entry has the cave-like appearance of the Richardsonian Romanesque style. The bow front, heavy cornice, and window caps with keystone motif are decorative features of the Colonial Revival style. Another classical feature is the brick facade broken by a stringcourse.

(15)

35 Church Street
1913

An excellent 'example of the Neoclassical style, the BayBank building also has Colonial Revival detail around the doorway. The front portico is pedimented with an attic story and smooth monumental Doric columns. A cornice block, an entablature, large pilaster, and keystone window caps are all reminiscent of the classical-style buildings of Imperial Rome. Beneath the pedimented front at the doorway are graceful, fluted Corinthian columns.

(16)

40 Church Street
c. 1871

Once part of "Doctors' Row" and home of Dr. Benjamin Church, this handsome Italianate building with a straight Mansard roof was radically changed in the early 1960s with the addition of a modern storefront. Looking above this addition, one can observe a Mansard roof with dormers, deep cornice brackets, an Italianate bay, and paired arched windows.

(17)

Out Main Street

43 Washington Street
1846 or earlier

Although a house in this location appears on the 1831 map, reference to this house first appears in 1846 when Francis Johnson, who owned the land, left a "new dwelling house" to his daughter. The Greek Revival details of the house, however, make it likely to have been built not long after 1830. Of special note is the front entry. The door is framed by partial sidelights, pilasters on either side, and a simple entablature above with an alternating tablet design in the frieze. The wide trim-boards on either end of the front facade are also characteristic of this period.

(1)

21 Washington Street
1840–1850

A fine example of high-style Greek Revival, this home was built by Deacon Nathan Brooks Johnson, a blacksmith. Johnson's shop was located next door and the ornamental iron grillwork that decorates the upper story of the full facade porch was probably made in his shop. Classical features are the temple front with a full pediment, a pair of fluted Corinthian columns, large Doric pilasters at the corners, and an entablature that encircles the house below the roofline. The off-center doorway is flanked by full sidelights with a transom across the top. In 1880 the house was purchased by Jacob Stanton, a grocer, who built the Stanton block in the town's center, and by whose name the house is now known.

(2)

81 Walnut Street
c. 1835–1850

This Gothic Revival–style house has the distinctive design features of steep roofline, paired gables, one-story, full-width porch, and a central projecting bay, but its vergeboard trim has been removed. Mr. Abijah Thompson, first president of the Winchester Historical Society, lived here between 1853 and 1867. He was a leather manufacturer and active in community affairs.

(3)

290 Highland Avenue
1856

Edward Brackett, artist, naturalist, and eccentric, built this octagon house based upon a planbook by Orson Fowler, who felt octagon houses were superior to square houses for increasing sunlight and eliminating dark and useless corners. There is no frame, but rather an interlocking series of octagons constructed out of a crib of boards. Brackett developed the plan for this house, which has four octagons of varying roof heights, with segments of others. The original board-and-batten design has been stuccoed. The overhang of the roofline, bracketing, and round-headed windows exhibit features of the Italianate style. Brackett maintained a commercial nursery on his property, raising fruits and vegetables.

(4)

305 Highland Avenue
1865

Moses A. Herrick built this house, which has features of the Tudor and Queen Anne periods. He was one of the first to build near the Fells and owned land from above Highland Avenue down to Main Street; Herrick Street was once the path to his farm. The house has a jerkin roof on the front gable, a bay, and a cross-gable. The house was stuccoed later. In 1912 the house was moved to its present site from 350 Highland Avenue, while its stone barn was moved to 11 Leslie Road and converted to a home. Herrick, treasurer of Nashua Iron and Steel Co., was a founder of the Winchester Savings Bank and served on the Winchester Board of Water Commissioners for forty years.

(5)

314–316 Highland Avenue
c. 1900

This house is in the Tudor style with half-timbering, grouped windows with small panes, and a combination of brick and stucco wall cladding. It was the home and studio of Herman D. Murphy, a local artist of some note who helped acquire the land along the Mystic Lakes on Cambridge Street for the Shu Shu Ga Canoe Club, which eventually became the Winchester Boat Club.

(6)

326 Highland Avenue
c. 1900

This eclectic house mixes Shingle, Tudor, Queen Anne, and Colonial Revival features. The corner tower has a Colonial Revival porch with Ionic columns, a balustrade, and large brackets. The gable dormers have half-timbering, finials, and solid decorated vergeboards. The roofline is dominated by a large corbeled chimney. Noteworthy are the diverse window treatments: simple double-hung 6-over-2, curved bay, small decorative oval, semi-hexagonal bay, and triple windows.

(7)

30 Mt. Pleasant Streeet
c. 1867

This multistoried Italianate house with a Mansard roof and four-story tower was first owned by William Carleton, a produce merchant at Boston's Faneuil Hall Market. The windows and widely overhanging eaves supported by decorative paired brackets are distinguishing features. Third-story windows have triangular pediments while the first floor paired windows are hooded. The first-floor L-shaped porch is marked by simple square posts, rounded arches, and decorative brackets with finials, all characteristic of the Italianate style.

(8)

10 Hillside Avenue
c. 1860–1870

Joshua Stone built this house before 1865 and it sold at auction to John C. Mason before 1875. Mason, among the first Boston businessmen to move to Winchester, served as a selectman and was a founder of the Methodist Church. This Italianate has tall, slender rectangular windows arranged in pairs, first-story bay window, arched-shaped dormer windows on the third story, and decorative brackets, all design features of this style. Cornice brackets alternate between paired and single. Each story has a different window-crown design, the first story having a scroll-like broken pediment with an inverted fleur-de-lis in the center. The front entry has double-arched doors and elaborate square piers.

(9)

4 Fairview Terrace
c. 1834

Although this house reflects architectural trends of the late-19th-century Colonial Revival style, it was built much earlier on a plot of land sold by Abijah Thompson to John Symmes in 1833. Originally built "as a store and shoe manufactory" on the present site of 417 Main Street, its land was later divided into house lots on newly created Fairview Terrace, and the house was moved. It was probably at that time, the early 1890s, that the Colonial Revival features of full-width porch, hip roof, bay, and Palladian window were added.

(10)

420 Main Street
1877

William and Mary Simonds built this classic Italianate house on land owned by Harrison Parker. Their daughter, Cora, ran a millinery shop in the house before her marriage. Note the paired brackets under the eaves, the narrow rectangular windows with pedimented crowns, the two side bays with bracketed cornices, and the Mansard roof with its uncommon dormer rooflines. The distinctive front entrance with paired front doors and a single-story columned porch all contribute to the house's Italianate character.

(11)

417 Main Street
c. 1854

Gardner Symmes, a local builder, built and later sold this Italianate house to Alfred Winton, a Winchester lawyer and prominent financial backer of the Winchester Hospital. The widely overhanging eaves with decorative supporting brackets, the first-story bay on the right side with narrow rectangular windows, and the elaborate window crowns highlighting each window are contributing Italianate details of this house. The front entry with half-sidelights surrounding the door and the small portico supported by square columns with simple balustrading around the second-story balcony are other Italianate features. Above the front door the window is arched, as are the windows on the third-story side.

(12)

403 Main Street
c. 1837

This vernacular Greek Revival–style house is claimed to have been built in the eighteenth century, but there is no documentary evidence to indicate that it was built that early. The low-pitched gable roof and stone chimney support a later date of construction. It was built on property owned by the Black Horse Tavern and might have been used as a shoe-making shop, judging from the size and location of the back ell. It seems likely that the main house was added on to the front of the shoe shop.

(13)

387 Main Street
c. 1905

Set on a small knoll away from the street, the size of this Colonial Revival house is accentuated. The unusually large projecting central gable with gothic arch is perhaps the most prominent feature of the facade. It is hollowed out for a balcony under the roof and is supported by paired Ionic columns with a full balcony on the second level; another pair of first-story columns supports the second-story portico. Single columns span the rest of the first-story porch; the two corner ones have Ionic capitals while the others resemble Doric capitals. The balustrades on both porches have intricate patterns with Queen Anne details. On the seond-story right side is a unique window that has a swan's-neck pediment, while on the left side the opposing window has an elaborate Gothic arch with Ionic columns on either side.

(14)

384 Main Street
c. 1841

John Coates, a prolific builder in this neighborhood, built this Greek Revival house. The plain entablature, simple fluted Doric columns and full first-story portico give this house its Greek Revival character. The centered front entrance with its fanlight and half sidelights are also typical of this style. Residents have included Reverend William Eustis, the second minister of the First Congregational Church; Joseph Hovey, the druggist and apothecary who also became the first town clerk; and Dennis Winn, who owned the first livery stable in town.

(15)

379 Main Street
c. 1840–1846

First bought by Hervy Wilbur, "an Orthodox preacher and lecturer on astronomy," this Greek Revival house was then sold to Charles Hubbard, a portrait painter and state senator. It originally included a stable, a large lot of land, and extensive gardens featuring grapevines and red and black cherry trees. The triangular pediment over the small single-story portico supported by round Doric columns, and partial sidelights on either side of the front entrance attest to the Greek Revival character of this house. However, the paired brackets under the eaves are more reminiscent of the Italianate style.

(16)

8 Prospect Street
1880/1896

This large Queen Anne house incorporates many architectural features to make it a distinctive structure. The expansive front entry wraparound porch with columns and fine spindlework are typically Queen Anne. The asymmetrical shape of the house and the complex irregularities of the roof are also features of this style. Also, numerous small and large bays on every level of the house add interest to the appearance. Preston Pond, the owner from 1896–1945, was treasurer of Dennison Manufacturing Company and owned several other properties in this immediate area. He razed the derelict Black Horse Tavern, which he owned at the time.

(17)

12 Prospect Street
c. 1886

This imposing residence combines the complexity of Queen Anne shapes and form with the formality of the Colonial Revival style to create an unusual-looking house. The front entry has wide sidelights and fluted columns on either side of the door. The porch with round Ionic columns in front and square columns on the left is a fine example of a Colonial Revival porch. The two main gables, however, are of special interest as one gable is in the Queen Anne style and the other in Colonial Revival. The Queen Anne section has a two-story, three-sided bay with latticed stick work design topped by fish-scale shingles in the gable end; a finial; and a very tall, paneled chimney. A noteworthy Colonial Revival feature is the two-story rounded bay with a Palladian window on the third level.

(18)

16 Prospect Street
1888

William Belcher built this three-story Shingle-style house at the same time that his brother Fred built 14 Prospect in the same style. William was the proprietor of W. M. Belcher and Company, a "manu-factory of caligraph writing machines." A fine example of a Shingle-style house, it exhibits different patterns of shingling on the bays, main surfaces, and dormers. The steeply pitched roof; asymmetrical facade; and windows that are either mul-tipaned above and double-paned below or single surrounded by smaller panes are also typical elaborations of the Shingle style.

(19)

366 Main Street
c. 1853

Although the first-story brick front is a modern alteration, the paired brackets, low-pitched roof, and small entry porch with square posts are original to this house's Italianate style. John Coates built this house in addition to a dozen others along Main Street. Among its various owners were Lewis Parkhurst, a principal of Winchester High School, and Thomas Lawson, who owned the property from 1897 to 1921. Lawson, a copper mag-nate, was a striking figure who drew much attention when he rode through town with the horses he bred.

(20)

346 Main Street
c. 1844

Also built by John Coates, this Italianate-style house was altered later. It had a se-ries of owners between 1844 and 1866 when James F. Dwinell, founder of a cof-fee import company and participant in town affairs, bought the property and had a Queen Anne overlay built onto the basic structure. While the double, paneled front-entry doors, low-pitched roof, widely overhanging eaves, and cen-tral second-story bay with narrow rectan-gular series of windows are evidence of the Italianate style, the full width, one-story porch with decorative spindlework ornamentation gives this house likeness to the Queen Anne style. The dentils and wide trim band beneath the eaves with the decorative frieze reflect the classical influence on this house.

(21)

336 Main Street
c. 1851

Another John Coates house, this was probably built in the Italianate style, then modified later. It has simple 2-over-2 windows, elaborate windowframes, and paired rectangular windows on the third level with different-shaped pedimented crowns. The paired window in the center has a rounded broken pediment unlike the two single windows on either side. A Mansard roof was added later and a Colonial Revival porch added still later. Of visual interest are the wood siding scored to resemble stone with quoins, the large balustraded portico with paired columns, and the full-length sidelights on either side of the front entrance. The original owner, Aaron D. Weld, was a town officer and paymaster during the Civil War.

(22)

319 Main Street
c. 1889

This Colonial Revival house has several features that contribute to its stately appearance. The fanlight over the front entrance and the sidelights draw attention to the front entry. The window above is framed by pilasters and by an oversized broken-scroll pediment and a projecting balcony. The symmetry of the front facade is typically Colonial Revival, as are the central entrance and evenly spaced 2-over-2 windows on both sides. The noteworthy feature here is the house's four-columned, full portico, added in 1923, with a balustrade and modillion blocks.

(23)

6 Madison Avenue
1907

This distinguished-looking Tudor-style house was the home of William Beggs of the family who owned the Beggs and Cobb Tannery on Swanton Street. The asymmetrical front, multiple gables, second-story overhang and half-timbered construction make this a house of typical Tudor design. Other characteristic features are the grouping of windows; the small window area in relation to the total wall area; the medieval arch leading to the front entrance; and the expansive side bays.

(24)

13 Madison Avenue
c. 1865

This Mansard house was first owned by Louis Goddu, an inventor and industrialist, who began the Goddu Sons Metal Fastening Company. He became the patriarch of a family of 13 children who settled in houses near his own. Number 12 Madison Avenue was built by Goddu for his daughter; 18 Chestnut Street and 2 Goddu Avenue were also family houses. The dual-pitched hip roof with dormer windows on its steep lower slope are distinguishing marks of the Mansard style. The decorative coupled brackets beneath the eaves, molded upper and lower cornices, and decoratively colored fish-scale roof shingles also distinguish this house. A Colonial Revival porch supported by Doric columns wraps around the house.

(25)

6 Goddu Avenue
1890

Like so many others in the immediate vicinity, this house was built by Louis Goddu—in this case for his son Louis H. Goddu, who worked for his father as a machinist. Although similar in form to 18 Chestnut Street and 2 Goddu Avenue, which were also constructed by Goddu, this Queen Anne does not have the second-story gable directly above the front door as do the other two homes. It does have the distinctive classical fluted columns like 18 Chestnut Street, but here they are supported by tall concrete pedestals. Typical design features of the Queen Anne style seen here are the different wall textures and the wraparound porch.

(26)

230 Main Street
c. 1817

This brick-ended Federal house has been owned by the Symmes family since its construction. Marshall Symmes, the first owner, was a blacksmith who kept a shop at the corner of Main and Bacon Streets. This house was built nearby in preparation for his marriage to Relief Stowell the following year. The high chimneys at four corners and the five openings across the front of the house, above and below, call attention to the symmetry of the house. The 6-over-6 windows and the front entrance with elliptical fanlight and partial sidelights are other indications of the period of this house. The small front-entry portico with its classical detail is also common to this style. Across the street, at 233 Main Street, is Marshall Symmes's tenant house, built by him in 1881 on the corner of the grounds of his estate.

(27)

212 Main Street
c. 1807

The oldest Symmes house in Winchester, this too is in the Federal style. It was built by Deacon John Symmes, son of the Revolutionary War veteran John Symmes, in what was then part of Medford. Symmes's wife ran the first formal school in Winchester from this house. Although the eave balustrade was removed and a front porch added that hides the entrance, this clapboard house still retains several distinctive features of the Federal style. They include the 6-over-6 windows aligned horizontally and vertically in symmetrical rows, and a hip roof, a feature common to New England Federal-style houses.

(28)

86 Main Street
c. 1872

James Russell first owned this Mansard-style house. He was a well-known market gardener and a charter member of the Boston Market Gardeners Association. Distinctive features include the Mansard roof with dormer windows, eaves with decorative brackets below, molded cornices binding the lower-roof slope above and below, simple windows, and a stone chimney and porch supports that display patterned edging. The L-shaped porch with rounded, grouped support posts are similar features to those used in Italianate houses of the same period.

(29)

8 Grove Street
c. 1854

This fine Italianate house was built by Thomas Prentiss Ayer, who came to Winchester around 1850 and took part in town government. The widely overhanging eaves with decorative paired brackets and caps over the long, narrow windows are clearly Italiante. The front entry porch, however, dates from 1920 and displays Colonial Revival influences such as the supporting columns, balustrading, fanlight, and sidelights.

(30)

7 Grove Street
c. 1914

An imposing Georgian Revival house with rich architectural details, this house's clear classical influences include the columned half-round entrance portico with balustrading above, and the decorative modillioned cornice. The one-story side wing with its flat roof; the broken pediments on the third-story dormer windows; and the symmetrical facade with center entrance and five openings above and below are frequent features of this style. The brick masonry is more common among the high-style Georgian Revivals than among the vernacular examples.

(31)

39 Oak Knoll
1893

Situated on a knoll bought from the daughter of Luther R. Symmes, the house was built by Lewis Parkhurst, who came to Winchester in 1881 to serve as principal of the high school. "Oak Knoll" combines Queen Anne and Colonial Revival architectural features to create an unusual residence. Simple Doric columns on the sweeping front porch and careful detailing around the front door, including a magnificent fanlight and sidelights, are reminiscent of the Colonial Revival style. The expansive porch, however, with decorative spindlework balustrading on the first and second levels, and the steeply pitched roof with an irregular shape, are marks of the Queen Anne style. Of particular interest is the varying window treatment. First- and second-story windows are primarily 1-over-1 with some arranged in bays of three, while the third level has arched dormer windows with decorative keystone detailing above.

(32)

26 Grove Street
c. 1835–1843

This fine example of a Greek Revival house is strikingly similar to the house at 384 Main Street built by the local builder John Coates. The detailing around the front entrance, including the transom and sidelights and the full-width porch supported by Doric columns, reflect this style. The perfectly simple, wide trim-board at the roofline is also characteristic. It stood originally near the corner of Main Street and Mystic Valley Parkway and was moved when the land was sold to Harrison Parker. Horace Hatch, a builder, was the first owner and in 1859 John Bacon, son of the felt manufacturer Robert Bacon, bought the house, perhaps to rent to his factory employees.

(33)

6 Mystic Valley Parkway
c. 1830

This transitional Federal-style house with Greek Revival overtones was built by John Cutts for Robert Bacon, who came to Winchester in 1824 to establish a felt mill in the former Symmes Mill on the lower Aberjona River. The windows placed close to the eaves with 6-over-6 panes are characteristic of the earlier Federal period. However, the front entry, the small portico supported by Doric columns, and the transom light above the door are marks of the Greek Revival style. The half sidelights, however, are more common to the Federal style than to the Greek Revival style. The decorative quoins on the sides of the front facade and the brick ends rising to form a parapet wall with a double chimney are also Federal in style, as is the service ell.

(34)

60 Lloyd Street
1854

Although situated on a small corner lot, this large Italianate originally stood at the corner of Main Street and Mystic Valley Parkway where the Unitarian Church now stands. It was built on land purchased by Harrison Parker, who founded the firm of Parker and Palmer, manufacturer of veneers and fancy woods. Its nearly flat roof with heavy projecting cornice has beautiful paired double-scroll brackets supporting the cornice. Some windows have rounded crowns, others simpler caps, but all have bracketing at the base. A stringcourse separates the first and second stories, and there are small square lights in the entablature below the roofline. Some of the Italianate features have been lost, however. In 1929 the top floor of the tower was removed and the front entry was completely enclosed.

(35)

27–29 Mystic Avenue
c. 1870

This vernacular house with Mansard features is half of a row of tenant housing built by Alexis Cutting in the 1870s for workers at his lumberyard, located on what is now Manchester Field. In 1893 it was divided and the other half moved to 9–11 Cutting Street. The decorative brackets beneath the eaves, the Mansard roof, the dormer windows with rounded window crowns on the third level, and the full-width porch are all distinguishing features of this house.

(36)

5 Mystic Avenue
1852

Originally located at 354 Main Street,
this Greek Revival house belonged to Arthur Whitney, a leading industrialist in
Winchester who, along with his father,
Joel Whitney, made machinery for the
veneering and leather tanning trades. The
simple front facade with plain wide trim-
board at the top of the second level and
the fluted, round Doric columns supporting a full-width porch extending along
one side wall are associated with this
style. The gentle pitch of the roof and
the prominent pediment on the third
level with a center window are of note.

(37)

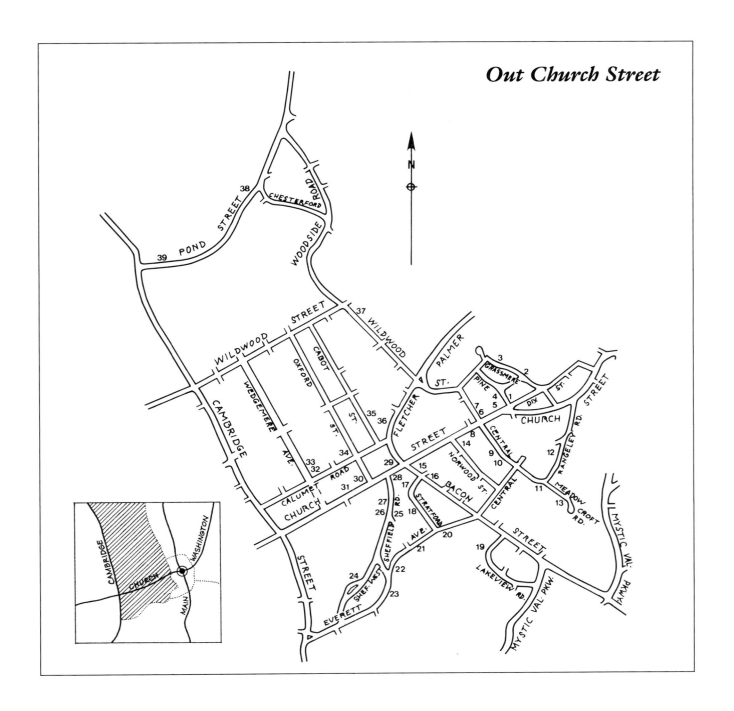

Out Church Street

37 Dix Street
c. 1897

This simple Colonial Revival clapboard house has a two-story gambrel-roof front connected to another gambrel-roof extension. The front facade is typically symmetrical: three gabled dormers with triangular pediments sit over rectangular windows on the second story. The smaller paired central windows are matched on the first floor by the entrance door. A full front porch with wide cornice and tapering Doric columns completes the front. Dentil molding and modillions under the eaves add some decorative interest. Also note the side projecting bay with strong Greek Revival elements. This house was built for William Firth, known for his development of the Grassmere-Pine-Glengarry area.

(1)

9 Glengarry Street
1897

This Gothic Revival clapboard house overlooking Wedge Pond was part of the Grassmere-Pine-Glengarry "Firth Development." It is in the centered nonparapeted gable style. The open rake eaves with exposed rafters and purlins provide decorative elements on all rooflines. First-floor bay windows add asymmetrical massing complemented by the cutaway-corner porch entrance. Typical diamond-paned windows are found with multipaned-over-1 windows in almost exuberant placement.

(2)

11 Grassmere Avenue
1865

Extensive additions and alterations have been jumbled together in this large, cross-gabled Gothic Revival–style cottage that jauntily overlooks Wedge Pond. Gingerbread ornamentation is prominent on the vergeboards under the eaves surmounted with a decorative finial. One-story bay windows on both the first and second stories increase the complex massing, as does the large one-story enclosed side addition. Windows are predominately rectangular. Some have typical drip-mold window crowns, and one diamond-shaped window accents the front gable. This clapboard house was built by Charles Curtis, owner of land and a nearby estate on Curtis Street, and later owned by the developer William Firth.

(3)

Neighborhood Walking Tours and Architectural Survey

2 Pine Street
c. 1876

This large Italianate home was built by Charles Conant, who worked for a Boston mirror manufacturer. His son was secretary to General John M. Corse (174–176 Mystic Valley Parkway) during the time that this famous Civil War hero was Postmaster for the city of Boston. The Italianate features seen in this home include the rounded paired windows in the dormers, the deep overhang with brackets, window caps, pilasters, and the squared posts supporting the roof of the entryway.

(4)

59 Church Street
1873

Around 1890 this Queen Anne–style house was acquired by David N. Skillings, whose estate was across Church Street. The asymmetrical porch with its square columns and brackets and modillion trim mark this as a Queen Anne. Note the flower-medallion motif on the third-story gable and repeated in the gable over the porch entry. A delicately carved decoration is also on the third-story gable.

(5)

1 Wildwood Street
1889

In 1888 John B. Rhodes, a broker, purchased the Rand estate at the corner of Church and Wildwood Streets, and the house was moved back to become 3 Wildwood Street. This unusual brick and shingle Queen Anne has varied shapes and styles of windows. Some have lintels that are arched, and some are flat with dentil moldings. There is decorative brickwork on the bay and the chimneys. Attractive landscaping adds to the overall charm of the site.

(6)

3 Wildwood Street
1843

Reportedly built by Gardner Symmes, business owner and builder during the railroad boom, this house was later owned by Elisha D. Bangs, president of the Boston Stock Exchange; it was probably a tenant house for its owners. A side-entrance Greek Revival with an L-shaped porch, it has floor-to-ceiling first-story windows with capped lintels, pilasters at the coners, and fluted Doric columns.

(7)

Corner of Church and Central Streets, Church of the Epiphany
1904

The first Episcopal Church services were held in a hall in the Brown and Stanton Block in the Center in 1882. In 1893 the present parcel of land was purchased and by Ocotober 1904 the cornerstone of the Gothic-style church was laid. The square tower was added in 1940. F. Patterson Smith, a Winchester resident, was the architect; he skillfully placed a piece of stone finial detail from the Winchester Cathedral (England) in the opening above the credence.

(8)

9 Central Street
c. 1880

Herbert S. Underwood, managing editor of the *Boston Advertiser & Record,* was the owner of this home from 1911–1953. It has the asymmetrical form of a Queen Anne, with bays and a full-width porch, but has Colonial Revival details such as Ionic columns, modillions, and a Palladian window. In addition, there are diamond-paned windows and stained glass windows reportedly from the original Congregational Church. Note that on the left side is a second-story sleeping porch and on the right side is an interesting scroll frieze on the bay.

(9)

15 and 17 Central Street
c. 1870

Numbers 15 and 17 Central were originally built as one house and divided in 1916, when number 17 was moved to its present location. The original owner was William H. Kinsman, a mariner. Later owners were Samuel J. Elder, a lawyer and Winchester's representative to the state legislature, and Samuel W. McCall, who later became governor of Massachusetts. Number 15 is stucco and has interesting window treatments: leaded glass windows at the entryway, arched windows in the dormers, a round third-story window, and balustrades on a window on the left side. Number 17 is of clapboard construction and has intricate dentil moldings, paired columns, an arched window on the right side, and a Palladian window on the left side.

(10)

38 Rangley Road
c. 1876

This home was built by David N. Skillings on the grounds of his estate and was the home of a famous Boston attorney, Samuel Elder. Mr. Elder represented Mary Baker Eddy and the Christian Science Church and represented the United States government at the Hague. The house is a panel-brick Queen Anne with red and black patterns in the brick and a handsome porch that has a balustrade and brackets with a design cut into them by jig saw.

(11)

19 Rangeley Road
c. 1885

Originally the stable for the David N. Skillings estate this structure once stood near the entrance to Rangeley Road. It was moved and converted to this imposing Colonial Revival–style home in 1902. There are many features of the Colonial Revival style that are present in this house: its symmetry, hip roof with three gabled dormers, large windows, a columned entryway with wide doorway, elliptical fanlight over the door and full sidelights. The building has a patio across the front and side porches with a balustrade at their roofline.

(12)

9 Meadowcroft Road
c. 1876

David N. Skillings built this Queen Anne house, one of three similar styles in panel brick on his Rangeley estate (see 2–6 and 38 Rangeley Road.) Interesting features here are the decorative wood trusses in gables that have both vertical and horizontal siding. Oversize brackets support the trusses, smaller ones support deep eaves, and brackets are used again on the square posts on the porch. Note the brick arches crowning the windows and the darker brick stringcourse defining the stories.

(13)

4 Norwood Street
c. 1856

This vernacular Italianate was the home of Kenelum Baker from 1856 to 1885. Mr. Baker was a carpenter who was active in Winchester and was responsible for the design of one of the early schools. The second owner, Henry C. Miller, lived in the house until 1919. He was also an active participant in local affairs. Besides political activity Mr. Miller was a founder of the Winchester Electric Light Company. The one-and-one-half story home features a center gable with rounded window. There are also the rectangular bays of the style that contain paired windows.

(14)

91 Bacon Street
c. 1877

This vernacular clapboard house has a front gable, wide cornerboards and cornices, and symmetrical window massing. The windows and door surrounds show Greek Revival influence while the porch and one-story bay windows reflect Italianate styling. An old photo shows an Italianate porch on the left that was removed and a part of it used for the present entrance porch. The heavy cornice was put across the top to form a pediment. Stephen Holt, the original owner, probably built it as rental property. An ordained minister, he had to give it up because of voice failure. He became an active Congregationalist and went into the mahogany milling business with his father-in-law, Henry Cutter.

(15)

89 Bacon Street
c. 1871

This large clapboard house is prodomi-
nately in the vernacular Greek Revival
style. The front-gabled roof is highlighted by a pedimented cornice with
dentil molding, a detail that continues on
the main house. The wide corner boards
serve as support, completing the Greek
temple form. Windows are usually single
with simple surrounds and a pedimented
cap. The Doric-columned one-story
porch with widow's walk completes the
front with the porch entablature continu-
ing on the sides of the house. Other features include cross-gabled side extensions,
a two-story, three-sided bay, and very
unusual twin crossed-gabled roof on the
north side. The original owner, Captain
John Bradford, was a warden whose
wife, Jane, was one of only twenty-five
women in Winchester entitled to vote on
the school question.

(16)

3 Stratford Road
c. 1901

A Phineas Nickerson-built house it has a
feature found in several of his other
houses—a long Doric-columned porch
with a bay at one end (see 92 and 94
Church Street). Under the deep eaves are
modillion and dentil decoration. Tall
bases supporting triple columns flank the
entryway, which has a large round-win-
dowed door. On the third-story is a
round diamond-paned window between
the hip-roof dormers. A second-story
sleeping porch is on the right.

(17)

11 Stratford Road
1913

Originally a carriage house, it was converted to a residence in 1938. It is characterized by a large, steep roof topped by
a small cuploa and has irregularly-placed
hip-roof dormers. A projecting three-
sided bay with a conical tower stands
near the house's outstanding feature, a
large arched, double entranceway with
the arch repeated by a curved overhang
supported by large brackets.

(18)

5 Lakeview Road
c. 1896

The symmetrical front facade of this Colonial Revival has gabled dormers flanking a central gabled bay, which has diamond-paned windows. Surmounting them is a fan window with keystone, echoing the side Palladian windows. Fluted Ionic pilasters are at the ends of the house while fluted Doric pilasters are at the entryway. A full-front porch has short, half-fluted Doric columns on tall shingled bases. The garage has a turntable and two stained-glass windows from the First Congregational Church when it was enlarged. The builder of this house was a Mr. Alexander who worked on the church's expansion.

(19)

8 Everett Avenue
c. 1879

Joseph Foxcroft Cole, a famous landscape artist, some of whose paintings are in the Boston Museum of Fine Arts, was the first to build on what is now Everett Avenue. Adelaide, his daughter and a portrait painter, was sketched by Winslow Homer during his visit to his friend's new home in the spring of 1879. The style is Colonial Revival with a slightly extended second-story bay and a wide entryway that has Doric double columns through which can be seen an elliptical fanlight window.

(20)

14 Everett Avenue
1906

This was the home of Roland H. Sherman, lawyer and judge, who served as Winchester's town counsel in 1919. The main emphasis in Colonial Revival houses is on entrances and windows, which in this house are highlighted to a fine degree. Pilasters outline a first-story entryway that has glass sidelights and a second-story window with a broken-scroll pediment. Quoins decorate the ends of the facade.

(21)

24 Everett Avenue
1899

A stucco-and-brick Colonial Revival–style house designed by F. Patterson Smith for his neighbors, the Everett Chadwick family. Mr. Chadwick, a patent attorney, wanted to move out of Boston to the country and chose this little-developed street. His son Harrison Chadwick who still occupies the home, was a state representative to the House from 1947 to 1974 and moderator of Town Meeting for sixteen years. Attention is drawn to the clean lines of the entryway with its brickwork, attractive fanlight window, wrought-iron balcony, and pediment.

(22)

30 Everett Avenue
1899

F. Patterson Smith, graduate and later dean of the Harvard Graduate School of Design, built this house for himself in a style similar to an English country home. The classical front entry has a balustraded balcony where quoins are centered and then repeated at every corner of the house. Two styles of lintels can be observed above the windows. Castellations run along the roofline at one end, and there is interesting spindlework on the service entry.

(23)

11 Sheffield West
1910

This early 20th-century home is an excellent example of the Bungalow style. Especially popular between the two world wars this style is not as much evident in Winchester as it is in some of the surrounding communities. It is a one-and-one-half-story home with a roof that slopes low over the porch, which is an integral feature of the structure rather than an attachment to it. The roof has a single dormer. There are exposed rafter ends and oversized brackets. The porch is supported by simple classic columns.

(24)

12 Sheffield Road
1898

This Blaikie/Nickerson home was originally owned and occupied by Oren C. Sanborn before the construction of his estate at 15 High Street in 1907. An imposing Shingle-style home, it has many Colonial Revival style features common to other houses on this street. There is a hip roof with large shed dormers and a deep overhang with exposed modillions. The porch has a series of arches supported by paired columns and intervening balustrade. The symmetry is somewhat broken by the porte-cochere that continues to reflect the decorative features of the home.

(25)

9 Sheffield Road
1898

This Blaikie/Nickerson building is an excellent example of the Shingle style with numerous Colonial Revival features. The steep hip roof has the oversized dormers of the Colonial Revivial style with curving swan's-neck pediments. There is the wide overhang to the roofline and exposed modillions. The home has lovely bay windows and grouped columns on the porch. A balustrade on the porch roof has decorative urns on its posts.

(26)

7 Sheffield Road
1898

Several of the large homes in this neighborhood were the product of the architect-builder team of Dexter Blaikie and Phineas Nickerson. This home is in the Colonial Revival Style. It is a two-and-one-half-story structure with a hip roof that has a large five-sided dormer. There are modillions on the deep overhang of the roof. The house has corner pilasters and a porch with paired Colonial Revivial columns and balustrade. A nice feature of this structure is its Palladian window and large entryway.

(27)

94 Church Street
1895

Built by Stillman Snow, a master mariner, on land that had once been a baseball field. Typical of the Shingle style, it has simple massing with some variety provided by attractive detailing. A towered bay has a conical roof matched by smaller pointed dormer roofs. Rising from the stone foundation is a full-width porch that ends in a octagon, similar to the porch at 92 Church Street, both having been built by Phineas Nickerson.

(28)

93 Church Street
1904

Much of the Wedgemere/Wyman Plains area was developed by Phineas Nickerson, a retired sea captain, who built and lived in this Tudor-style house. It was reported that he made 1,200 round-trips to Philadelphia in his thirty years with the Boston & Philadelphia Steamship Co. Built of stucco with stick trim, the house displays simulated half-timbering on the four front gables and on the sides. Tall chimneys dominate the steep slate roof.

(29)

105 Church Street
1908

Unique among its more traditional neighbors, this Mission-style house has roof parapets on three sides and even on the carriage house. The red tile hip roof has widely overhanging eaves, repeated in the porch roof, which is supported by large, square piers. The pink stucco covering, arched windows, varied window-pane patterns, and balconies give this house its Spanish flavor.

(30)

111 Church Street
1893

Situated on land that was part of the Wedgemere Syndicate, this Colonial Revival house was built for William B. French, a lawyer. The balustrated porches have triple and double columns and finial post decorations. Palladian windows grace all sides while other windows are capped by lintels; those at the entryway are leaded. The pedimented dormers have dentil moldings.

(31)

29 Calumet Road
1894

This house is an excellent example of the Shingle style, which aimed for the effect of a complex shape enclosed within a smooth shingled surface, thus unifying the irregular outline. The basic form here is a hip roof with cross-gambrel gables. Simple gabled dormers add mass to the multilevel eaved roof. Two round towers, one story and two-and-one half story, also add to the complex massing. These are matched by a porte-cochere and a full side porch, both supported by classical Ionic columns. Note the rusticated stone under the porte-cochere and the brick chimneys with rounded corners. Windows are characteristically multipaned above two panes: there is also a decorative Palladian window over the front entrance. This house was built about 1894 for Augusta Boynton and her son William, who moved from their family farm on nearby Cambridge Street.

(32)

19 Wedgemere Avenue
1893

Several interesting features of this Colonial Revival–style house are the bowed front entry, the bowed windows above it, the patterned pilasters, and the curved, peaked dormers. There are Palladian windows on either end of the second story, the left has a narrow porch and the right is above a bay. The long porch with Doric columns extends to the side to form a porte-cochere. The former carriage house is now 21 Wedgemere Avenue, which was remodeled in 1984.

(33)

14 Oxford Street
c. 1898

This large home at the corner of Calument Road and Oxford Street, built and first lived in by the James W. Fitch family, is an excellent example of a Shingle-style home with Colonial Revival trim. The basic structure is a two-and-one-half-story building with a hip roof. There are oversized dormers with diamond windowpanes in the roof. The deep overhang has the modillions common to other turn-of-the-century styles. Its lovely porch has paired Colonial Revival columns.

(34)

15 Cabot Street
c. 1902

This shingled house was built in the Tudor style, which can be seen in the steep, slate hip roof, Gothic entrance details, and half-timbered twin gables. The unusual curved open porch on the second story provides additional ventilation to the front bedrooms and light to the staircase. With screens, it could have served as a sleeping porch, a popular feature in early 20th-century homes.

(35)

45 Fletcher Street
1889

Captain Phineas Nickerson bought the lot on which this Shingle-style house is built from William Boynton, who owned much of the land in Wyman Plains. Variety is the hallmark of the Shingle style and it is evident here. One side has a two-story tower with dome-shaped roof and finial, and the other side has an octagonal porch, which was enclosed in the 1930s. The pediments have painted decorations, and the shingles have varying patterns with sawtooth edges at some ends. The windows also vary in style, and there is a set of beautiful stained-glass windows in the stairwell.

(36)

41 Wildwood Street
1888

Built on land once owned by Samuel W. Twombley whose property ran the length of Wildwood Street to Cambridge Street, this Queen Anne–style house reflects the trend from farmhouse to suburban residence. Decorative detailing is seen in the fish-scale shingles, the eave brackets, and the bas-relief design in the porch pediment. This house is set apart from others of the Queen Anne style by the porch spindlework and the curved second-story windows.

(37)

136 Pond Street
c. 1865

Pond Street has many structures that in the nineteenth century were the homes of workers. People who were carpenters, masons, farmers, and shoemakers lived in this neighborhood. These vernacular houses appear in the various styles of the early Victorian age. This one is a small one-and-one-half-story dwelling in the Mansard style. The roof, with its concave curving lines, covers a deep cornice. There are corner boards and a three-sided bay window.

(38)

26 Pond Street
c. 1850

This home is an excellent example of a vernacular Greek Revival–style building. The gable end faces the street and has returning eaves over an entablature and side pilasters. The effect of this feature is to leave the observer with the impression of a pediment. The entablature continues to run along the length of each side of the building. There is a one-story porch supported by fluted Doric columns. The doorway is in the lovely Greek Revival style of full sidelights and transom. The wing to the right of the home was an addition that incorporated the Greek motif of the basic house.

(39)

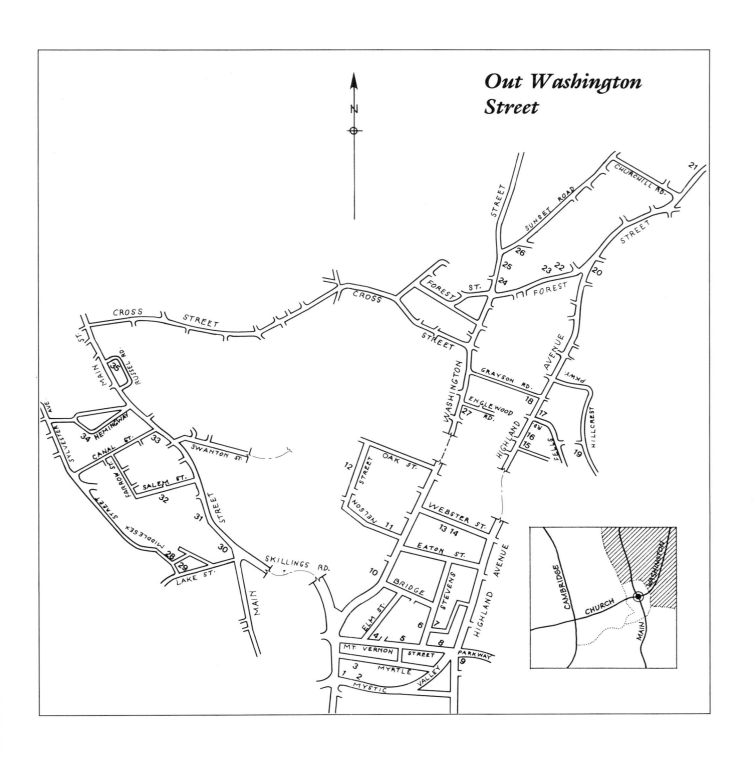

Out Washington Street

174–176 Mystic Valley Parkway
1854

This Italianate residence was built in 1854 and has the deep roof overhang, paired brackets, bay windows, and squared porch posts typical of the style. Its exterior siding was much altered in modern times. Built by David N. Skillings, a community leader in banking and development, the home was acquired by the Civil War General John M. Corse in 1886. During Sherman's brilliant drive on Atlanta in 1864, General Corse was a major contributor to the eventual Union victories around that city. After the war this western general moved east to become the postmaster for Boston and a resident of Winchester until his death in 1893.

(1)

180 Mystic Valley Parkway
c. 1855

This Italianate house in the style of a Tuscan villa is interesting for the scalloping along the cornices, heavy paired bracketing, window trim, and central cupola. Dr. John French lived here from 1910 to 1918 and used the first floor as his office. The kitchen was originally in the basement, where an existing brick oven bears the date 1854.

(2)

5 Myrtle Street
c. 1840

This home is the survivor of a pair built in the early 1840s and located in the area of the present Town Hall and Library; it was moved to its present site in 1887. The house's asymmetrical lines and cut-out vergeboards that frame the gables and lead to the acorn drops at the peaks are Gothic in style, as is in the front gable window with pointed arch and wooden tracery. The structure itself is essentially Greek Revival in style, with corner pilasters and a doorway framed by full sidelights. A porch to the left was added in the Queen Anne period, as attested to by its turned posts.

(3)

110 Mount Vernon Street
1894

This 1894 Queen Anne was built as a home for the aged and continues to serve in that capacity. The style was chosen to blend in with other private structures in the neighborhood. It has a pyramidical roof, turreted tower, and the asymmetrical massing common to the Queen Anne style.

(4)

134 Mount Vernon Street
1884

Built in 1884 as a rental property by Joseph Shattuck, a local carpenter-developer, this home is in the Queen Anne style with a mixture of shingle and clapboarding. Features include solid vergeboards and stick work in the gable.

(5)

8 Stevens Street
c. 1850

This Carpenter Gothic cottage has a steep central gable and roof with vergeboards cut in an icicle pattern. The peaks of the gables are decorated with finials, and there is drip molding around the windows. The front entryway is a Colonial Revival porch added much later. The home was built by Samuel White, a founder of the Congregational Church and Winchester's first town treasurer. For comparison, note the acorn-drop vergeboard trim on 14 Stevens, a pattern unique in the town. This house is a transitional Gothic/Italianate.

(6)

7 Stevens Street
c. 1865

This home was first owned by Rev. Barrett, the minister of the Baptist Church from 1870 to 1874. Early in the twentieth century it was the home of Daniel Hawes, who came to Winchester in the mid 1870s to work for the grocer J. C. Stanton. In 1877 Daniel, with his brother, founded a livery and express company on Railroad Avenue, which became Kelley and Hawes Company. The structure is Mansard style with straight edges to the roof, which contains dormers. The brackets and other decoration, as with all Mansards, is Italianate. The elaborate porch with columns and balustrade was added later and is Colonial Revival in style.

(7)

158–160 Mount Vernon Street
1865

This Italianate-style house, built in 1865, originally faced Stevens Street but was turned about in 1916 by the Saltmarsh family, who have owned it ever since. The first owner was Salem Wilder, who was active in town affairs and was a general agent for the Elias Howe Sewing Machine Company. The house has the deep roof overhang, arched windows, squared front porch posts, and window trim common to the Italianate style.

(8)

221 Mystic Valley Parkway
1896

This 1896 home is an excellent example of the Colonial Revival style. Its stately symmetrical features include a large Palladian window, columned entryway with Ionic capitals, imposing pilasters with Corinthian capitals, and a hip roof with gabled dormers. Large front windows and an oversize doorway help identify it as a late-19th-century structure rather than an earlier Federal home. The house was originally built for William P. Greely, a successful coffee dealer who intended it for his daughter Addie. Her husband was a music teacher from Salem who eventually became curator of the Essex Institute in that city.

(9)

162 Washington Street
c. 1845–1850

The present convent of Saint Mary's Church is an excellent example of Italianate-style home built sometime between 1845 and 1850. The pyramid tower roof and the roofline of the gabled wings of the building feature oversized brackets. There are paired windows, some sporting arched detail, below the deep overhang of the roof. This lively villa-style house was built by Jerome B. Judkins, who purchased the farm that stretched from Washington to Main Street. He sold off house lots on Westley and Nelson Streets while living in this home until his death in 1889. Judkin's Pond at the base of the ridge the house dominated was filled in and became the site of the present Winchester High School. In 1903 the property was sold to the Catholic Church.

(10)

7–9 Nelson Street
c. 1870

This Mansard-style home has a concave roofline with three pedimented dormers on each side and at the front. There are large brackets at the cornice, and the porch has Italianate posts and brackets. Since its construction it has been vinyl-sided and remodeled into apartments.

(11)

68 Nelson Street
c. 1865

This vernacular Greek Revival–style home originally stood on lower Main Street near Washington Street. It was owned by Francis H. Johnson, a blacksmith, who with his brother, a resident at 21 Washington Street, established a shop that made tools for local tanneries and mahogany veneer mills. The house was later purchased and moved by Patrick Holland to Nelson Street and utilized as rental property for Irish laborers. It has a deep overhang to the roofline and the traditional Greek Revival doorway, but the porch is an addition from the Queen Anne period.

(12)

3–5 Webster Street
1889

Before extensive fire damage changed the lines of this lovely Queen Anne, it was far less symmetrical. To the left of the entrance rose a many-sided tower. A large center dormer and front and side gables broke the surface of a sharply pitched roof. Yet the front and side bays still display excellent paneling and large fan brackets at the roofline, attesting to their Queen Anne origins. Since the fire the lines of this 1889 home are more symmetrical, and the Colonial Revival porch is the dominant feature of the facade. Originally owned by Caroline Payne, until 1916 it was rental property; one of her tenants was Charles T. Main, founder of the Boston engineering firm of that name.

(13)

7 Webster Street
c. 1896

This is a striking Queen Anne house with a rambling front porch and paired Colonial Revival columns. Solid paneled vergeboards line the gabled ends of the steeply pitched roof and decorative bracketing frames the corners of the gables. Large decorative panelled bays extending upward for three stories and cutaway corners add to the features of this late-Victorian beauty. Built around 1896, this house was also owned by Caroline and George Payne as part of their rental property.

(14)

112 Highland Avenue
1893

Part of the extensive Hillcrest development of Arthur Wyman, this home was owned in the late 1890s by Edward Braddock, an inventor with numerous patents for tinning and galvanizing. A Shingle style with Colonial Revival decoration, it has a hip roof with dormers and gables. Below the deep overhang of the roof are bays and a porch with Colonial Revival columns. A porte-cochere on the right side of the house does not lead to a door.

(15)

108 Highland Avenue
1893

This is an imposing and interesting Shingle-style home with Queen Anne features including a tower, steep gables (with an oriel window in the front gable), and diamond windowpanes; the front porch has Colonial Revival-style columns. Built by the developer Arthur Wyman in 1893, it became the home of the Arthur French family in 1916.

(16)

94 Highland Avenue
1896

This imposing home was once owned by Charles Chapman, founder of the Chapman Spindle Manufacturing Company, once located on Main Street. It is in the Shingle style with decorative features of the Queen Anne and Colonial Revival styles. The round tower with conical roof, the rounded bay, and the bracketing come from the late-Victorian Queen Anne style. The Palladian window in the gable and columns on the porch are of the classical Colonial Revival style. The stained-glass window built into the chimney on the first floor is an interesting feature.

(17)

87 Highland Avenue
c. 1913

This Tudor, built around 1913, has typical half-timbering in the gable along with stick work and solid vergeboards. The first story and the porte-cochere are in fieldstone. Edward Comfort, an inventor, was the first owner of the home.

(18)

30 Hillcrest Parkway
c. 1911

Rufus Galusha, a real estate speculator who owned much land in the Hillcrest and Euclid Avenue area, had the house built for him in the Mission style, a style that began in California in the late 1800s and that was more commonly built in the Southwest. The Spanish influences are seen in the tile roof and the stucco exterior. Note also the curve motif repeated in the porch roof and the half-round windows of the tower facade. Other windows are in groups of three and four.

(19)

2 Highland Avenue
c. 1845

This may have been a Richardson home, as Mary Elizabeth Richardson of 224 Forest Street married Issac Kendall here in 1847. The first known owner of the Gothic Revival–style house was Francis Chisholm around 1854. His daughter lived in the house until 1921. The jigsaw trim of the vergeboards at the gable and on the dormers are indicative of its Gothic style.

(20)

224 Forest Street
c. 1837

Jason Richardson, a teamster, was said to have collected the stone for this unique home in his travels around the area. He was at one time or another a shoemaker, farmer, and clock cleaner in addition to his occupation of wagon driver. He was active in local politics and was a noted reformer. The home is in the vernacular Greek Revival style with the sidelights of that period and classical quoins at the corners. The roof with its shed dormer and the wing to the left were added at a later time.

(21)

Neighborhood Walking Tours and Architectural Survey

146 Forest Street
c. 1840

This home was probably a traditional "12 footer": one of the shoe shops commonly owned by area farmers to supplement their agrarian income during the winter. It probably belonged to the home at 142 Forest Street. It has the exterior decoration of the Greek Revival period with pilasters, entablature, and sidelights at the doorway, and simple corner boards.

(22)

142 Forest Street
c. 1854

The land for this home was a gift by Zachariah Richardson to his daughter Adeline and her husband Calvin Parker. It is a vernacular Greek Revival–style structure with corner boards, an overhang to the roofline and the typical sidelights and transom windows framing the doorway.

(23)

569 Washington Street
c. 1831

This five-across vernacular Federal–style home was built around 1831, and later had a front porch added and its exterior shingled. Originally owned by Jesse Richardson, it stands on part of the original land granted to Samuel Richardson in 1641. Jesse's son Samuel (seventh generation) was a hardworking farmer and teamster who resided in the house with his family until 1886. Number 118 Forest Street was originally the barn of Samuel Richardson's home. It was built between 1831 and 1854 and converted to this American Colonial home in 1919.

(24)

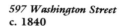

597 Washington Street
c. 1840

This property is the site of a 1794 school that was part of Richardson's Row and that later became a shoe shop before the present home was built from parts of the original foundation and structures. The earliest portions, including the right three window openings, date from the early Federal period, while the left three openings, including the door, are of later construction. The exterior trim and doorway are of the Greek Revival style.

(25)

7 Sunset Road
c. 1810–1830

This early vernacular home, built in the Federal period, was the residence of Zachariah Richardson in the 1860s. He was occupied in mill work, lath turning, and farming, and was a clerk in a Charlestown store. The original home was added on to and changed over the years and now has some Italianate features. When built, the structure was set back several hundred feet from the road, but due to the subsequent construction of homes closer to Washington Street this Richardson Row house now carries a Sunset Road address.

(26)

423 Washington Street
before 1854

This interesting one-and-one-half-story cottage represents two early Victorian styles. The rear ell is Gothic Revival, with steep gables and a square bay. The front is Greek Revival, with simple Doric columns on the porch and a Greek doorway (although the sidelights and transom have been covered over). The house was owned by Samuel Holton, a boot and shoe dealer, who was active as a selectman in town affairs. The exterior of this early Winchester home has been shingled.

(27)

3 Middlesex Street
c. 1830

This vernacular home was built around 1830 and was moved to this site around 1865. It is thought to have originally been a boathouse on the Middlesex Canal, which was about 250 feet away in the direction of the cemetery property. Early in the nineteenth century it was owned by Edward O'Connell, a currier employed in a nearby tannery. If one looks down Middlesex Street, away from Lake Street, a line of worker housing owned by the tannery is visible on the opposite side of the street. Most of Mr. O'Connell's neighbors were employed in the same industry.

(28)

57 Lake Street
c. 1860

This interesting Mansard with Italianate trim features a deep roof overhang and a tower with a concave Mansard roof topped by a finial. There is a square bay with paired windows common to this style, paired bracketing at the roofline, and three-sided arched windows. It was built by the carpenters Moses and James Mann. Number 61 Lake Street was the barn of this house until converted in 1878 to a home.

(29)

735 Main Street
c. 1831

This was the home of Andrew Cutter, who was employed in the mill of brothers Stephen and Henry, located nearby on Horn Pond Brook. Originally built for grinding grain, the mill was later used for picking and carding wool, manufacturing machines for splitting leather, and finally for sawing wood. In 1853 Andrew moved to Vermont and sold the house to a sawyer, probably employed in the Cutter mill. Henry Cutter's house at 760–762 Main Street was built around 1845, but is almost unrecognizable behind modern cladding and additions.

(30)

780 Main Street
c. 1845

Stephen Holt built this Italianate house, which has undergone unfortunate modernization. It was originally clapboard and one of a number of "Cutter Village" houses in the neighborhood. Holt married Nancy Wyman Cutter and was in business with her father Henry in the importing and milling of mahogany and exotic woods used in many area houses. The front entry has square columns surmounted by a balustraded balcony and an arched window. The widely overhanging eaves are supported by decorative brackets.

(31)

38–40 Salem Street
c. 1865

This vernacular Italianate-style home has bracketing on the doorway. It was built by George Hall, a maker of pianoforte cases. Between 1880 and 1924 it was rental property for workers employed in the nearby tanneries.

(32)

898 Main Street
c. 1870

Fronting Canal Street at the corner of Main is this simple, vernacular Italianate with gables and deep overhanging roof. It has heavy window caps, square chamfered posts on the front and side entries and a paneled chimney. It was built before 1876 by Charles Moseley, a leather manufacturer, who owned it until 1889 when Alex Moseley, a Swanton Street tanner, took it over. The Moseley factory became a famous Beggs and Cobb Tannery at the site of the present Parkview Condominiums on Swanton Street. Beggs and Cobb acquired the house and during their ownership rented it to their employees.

(33)

67 Hemingway Street
1840

This Gothic Revival has the vergeboards
and ornamental drops of that style. The
porch has since been enclosed; the left
wing was originally a stable. In 1875 it
was acquired by John W. Hemingway, a
milk dealer and lamplighter. Mr. Hemingway, for whom the street was named,
was a passionate temperance crusader.
He was appointed a special constable and
would use his authority to raid the local
"kitchen rum shops" and to stop the liq-
uor trade from coming from Woburn.

(34)

993 Main street
1841

This house was built in 1841 by Charles
Russell, who died a decade later. His
widow resided in the home with her son
James Russell, an active community
leader who served as an assessor, school
committeeman, and selectman. The imposing Greek Revival–style home was
built in the Federalist manner with a
five-opening facade and pedimented gable ends. The structure sits atop a slight
knoll and is set back from the street. Its
classical Greek Revival features include an
encircling entablature, corner pilasters,
Ionic fluted columns at the entryway,
and doorway framed by full sidelights
and transom window. At some time in
the modern period its clapboard siding
was replaced with asbestos shingling.

(35)

Appendix 1
Tracing Your House's History

To trace your house's history, begin by consulting a style guide to determine the approximate style and period of your house. You may use the drawings in Part III of this book as a starting point, or you may wish to use one of the guides listed below. With the guide in hand, look at the major elements of your house and compare them to the pictures and descriptions in the guide; note windows, rooflines, doors, siding, and chimneys in particular. Investigating such details as floorboards, walls, and roof construction, or the type of glass in your windows can often provide a more precise dating than a classification on the basis of the existing facade. It may also be possible to locate actual records or engineering drawings in local county or town offices, libraries, or historical societies. If you expand your research into the physical aspects of your house to include previous owners, you will also gain a sense of the social history of your neighborhood and the town as a whole.

Following is a bibliography and guide to local information sources that will assist you in researching an older home.

STYLE GUIDES AND PATTERN BOOKS

Bicknell, A.J. and William Comstock. *Victorian Architecture: Two Pattern Books.* NY: American Life Foundation, 1977.

Blumenson, John. *Identifying American Architecture, A Pictorial Guide to Styles and Terms, 1600–1945.* NY: Norton, 1981.

Downing, Andrew Jackson. *The Architecture of Country Houses.* NY: Dover, 1969.

Gottfried, Herbert and Jan Jennings. *American Vernacular Design, 1870–1940.* NY: Van Nostrand Reinhold, 1985.

McAlester, Virginia and Lee McAlester. *A Field Guide to American Houses.* NY: Knopf, 1984.

Scully, Vincent J. *The Shingle Style and the Stick Style.* New Haven: Yale University Press, 1971.

Whiffen, Marcus. *American Architecture Since 1780, a Guide to the Styles.* Cambridge, MA: MIT Press, 1969.

MUNICIPAL RESOURCES

Henry E. Simonds Memorial Archival Center, 15 High Street, Winchester, MA

The original forms and supporting documentation for the pre-1917 buildings survey are on file here and should be consulted first to see how much research has already been done on a house. Some of the special collections at the Archival Center are listed here.

Town directories of residents: incomplete holdings from 1874–present.

Annual Report of the Town of Winchester: 1850–present. Some early years include tax lists and vital records.

U.S. Census of Winchester (on microfilm): 1850, 1860, 1870, 1880, 1900.

Family files and genealogies.

Scrapbooks and photographs.

Atlases:

J.B. Beers Atlas of Middlesex County, Massachusetts. 1875.

G.H. Walker Atlas of Middlesex County, Massachusetts. 1889 edition; 1906 edition.

Sanborn Map Company. Insurance maps of Winchester, Massachusetts. 1916.

Maps:

1831, of Woburn, showing buildings.
1854, of Winchester, showing buildings.
1875, of Winchester, showing buildings.
1886, bird's eye view map of Winchester.
1898, bird's eye view map of Winchester.

Middlesex County Courthouse, 40 Thorndike Street, Cambridge, MA

The Registry of Deeds has original deeds for Winchester property and some plot plan maps. The Registry of Probate has on file the wills and inventories of estates.

Woburn Public Library, 45 Pleasant Street, Woburn, MA

Woburn town records, valuation, and tax lists are from the early 1700s, but not complete for all years.

Newspapers (on microfilm and indexed): *Woburn Advertiser,* 1871–1888 and *Woburn Grattan Echo,* 1811–1882.

Winchester Public Library, 80 Washington Street, Winchester, MA

Town directories of residents: 1874, 1895, 1904, 1914, 1916.

Annual report of the Town of Winchester: 1850–present. Some early years include tax lists and vital records.

Newspapers (on microfilm): *Woburn and Middlesex Journal,* October 1851–November 1906 (not indexed); *Winchester Star,* 1881–present (indexed); *Winchester Press,* October 1900–December 1902 (not indexed).

Winchester Record, published by the Winchester Historical and Genealogical Society, volumes 1–3, 1885–1887.

Chapman, Henry S. and Bruce W. Stone. *History of Winchester.* 2 volumes. Winchester, MA: Town of Winchester, 1975.

Pictorial History of Winchester. Theo P. Wilson, 1914.

Simonds, Henry E. *Winchester, Then and Now.* Woburn, MA: Woburn Daily Times and Chronicle, 1979.

Winchester Historical Commission. Survey of pre-1917 buildings. 11 volumes, 1979.

Appendix 2
Sources of Information on Preservation, Restoration, and Renovation

Following is a selected list of publications and organizations that are among the best sources of information available on old house preservation and restoration.

BOOKS AND PAMPHLETS

American Association for State and Local History, *Technical Leaflets,* Nashville: The Association. Discusses wood deterioration, brick and stone restoration, paint, color research, and other subjects in an understandable manner.

Athenaeum of Philadelphia, *Exterior Decoration, Victorian Colors for Victorian Homes,* Philadelphia: The Athenaeum, 1976. Excellent aid to selecting authentic house colors. Lithographs are keyed by number to chips of actual paint matched to 19th-century originals.

Eastlake, Charles L., *Hints on Household Taste, the Classic Handbook of Victorian Interior Decoration,* reprint of the 1878 edition, NY: Dover, 1986. Originally written to attract the general public to a simpler style of interior design. The English author, best known for his massive Gothic-style furniture, covers not only furniture, but also pottery, carpet patterns, metalwork, fabrics, and wall decorations.

Grow, Lawrence and Von Zweck, Dina, *American Victorian, Style and Source Book,* NY: Harper and Row, 1984. Interiors are selected from homes around the country that are *not* museum houses. Illustrations show how Victorian decors may be recreated using wallcoverings, floorcoverings, draperies, and furnishings. Sources for the products are listed.

Hanson, Shirley and Hubby, Nancy. *Preserving and Maintaining the Old Home,* NY: McGraw-Hill, 1983. A guide to restoring homes built from the 17th century to 1940. Advice on identifying styles and how to repair rather than replace.

Johnson, ed, *Old House Woodwork Restoration,* Englewood Cliffs, NJ: Prentice-Hall, 1983. A thorough treatment of the topic that includes background on tools, materials and wood finishes. Details the step-by-step process of repairing and refinishing all types of wood, inside and out.

Labine, Clem, *Old-House Journal Compendium: Renovating and Maintenance Ideas for the Antique House,* Brooklyn, NY: The Old-House Journal Corp., 1980. A collection of illustrated articles from the first years of publication of the Old-House Journal. Solid, how-to restoration information for the do-it-yourselfer.

Leopold, Allison K., *Victorian Splendor, Recreating America's 19th-Century Interiors,* NY: Stewart, Tabori, & Chang, 1986. Fine color photographs of interiors that one can simulate in contemporary homes or 19th c. originals. Lists suppliers.

Litchfield, Michael, *Renovation, a Complete Guide,* NY: Wiley, 1982. Well-illustrated guide to every aspect of renovation explained by master craftsmen. Sets forth the principles underlying each procedure to give an understanding of what has to be done and how to do it.

Living With Old Houses, Third Edition, Portland, ME: Greater Portland Landmarks, Inc., 1985. Written for new owner of an old house, it helps in recognizing styles, researching a house, and planning restoration. Also gives practical advice on hardware, lighting, paint, wallpaper, and more.

Maddex, Diane, ed., *All About Old Buildings, the Whole Preservation Catalog,* Washington, D.C.: Preservation Press, 1985. Excellent resource for locating all types of preservation information, whether it be on restoring a house, saving a town landmark, or researching the history of a building.

Moss, Roger and Winkler, Gail. *Victorian Exterior Decoration, How to Paint Your Nineteenth-Century American House Historically,* NY: Holt, 1987. Chapters on selecting colors, color placement, history of color use and why some colors are more appropriate than others for buildings of a particular age and style. Illustrations taken from archival paint company catalogs and photos of exemplary Victorian houses of today. Represented are four major paint companies with the thirty-four most common Victorian colors currently available.

The Old-House Journal Catalog, a Where-To-Buy-It Guide for the Pre-1930 House, Compiled by the editors of The Old-House Journal, Brooklyn, NY: The Old-House Journal Corp. Annual buyer's guide to over 10,000 hard-to-find restoration products and services.

Rusk, Katherine, *Renovating the Victorian House,* San Francisco: 101 Productions, 1981. Sourcebook on restoring houses in a sensitive manner. Chapters on architectural styles, construction, interior decoration, and gardens.

Seale, William, *The Tasteful Interlude, American Interiors Through the Camera's Eye, 1860–1917,* Nashville: American Association for State and Local History, 1981. Original photographs accompanied by informative captions give a glimpse of how primarily middle-class Americans decorated their houses in the period between the Civil War and WWI.

Stephen, George, *Remodeling Old Houses Without Destroying Their Character,* NY: Knopf, 1982. Outlines good qualities found in old houses and how to retain them with as little strain on the budget as possible. Aims for the liveable, unspoiled house.

U.S. National Park Service, Office of Archeology and Historic Preservation, *Preservation Briefs,* Washington, D.C.: Government Printing Office. A series of documents on topics such as cleaning and waterproofing masonry, repairing mortar joints, conserving energy, artificial siding, and exterior paint problems.

Wharton, Edith and Codman, Ogden Jr., *The Decoration of Houses,* NY: Norton, 1978. Originally published in 1902, this book became extremely influential on the contemporary design of interiors. Especially noteworthy is the section on the practical layout of the kitchen.

Winkler, Gail and Moss, Roger W., *Victorian Interior Decoration, American Interiors 1830–1900,* NY: Henry Holt, 1986. Profuse illustrations, taken from design books, trade catalogs, paintings and photographs, show how Victorians decorated their homes. Looks at the way walls, ceilings, woodwork, floors, and windows were treated in four chronological periods.

JOURNALS

Fine Homebuilding. Bi-monthly. 62 South Main Street, Box 355, Newtown, CT 06470.

Historic Preservation. Bi-monthly. National Trust for Historic Preservation. 1785 Massachusetts Avenue, N.W., Washington, D.C. 20036.

The Old-House Journal. Ten/yr. Old-House Journal Corporation, 69A Seventh Avenue, Brooklyn, NY 11217.

Victorian Homes. Quarterly. Renovators Supply, Inc. Millers Falls, MA 01349.

Boston Society of Architects, 320 Newbury Street, Boston, MA 02115. Offers evening classes for the general public on all aspects of architecture. Their bookstore at 66 Hereford Street has one of the largest selections in the country of books on architecture and related fields.

National Trust for Historic Preservation, 1785 Massachusetts Avenue, NW, Washington, D.C. 20036. A quasi-public organization funded by Congress to serve as a clearinghouse for preservation issues. It publishes *Preservation News* and *Historic Preservation.* The local regional office at 45 School Street, Boston, distributes free pamphlets and provides preservation services to nonprofit organizations in the Northeast.

Society for the Preservation of New England Antiquities, Harrison Gray Otis House, 141 Cambridge Street, Boston, MA 02114. An excellent source for help in answering technical questions on the best methods and newest techniques of restoration. They have a fine research library, sponsor special programs, and operate approximately 60 house museums.

Victorian Society in America (Boston Chapter), 137 Beacon Street, Boston, MA 02116. They sponsor field trips relating to Victorian life and architecture and publish a newsletter.

Winchester Historical Commission, 15 High Street, Winchester, MA 01890. A town-appointed committee that was established in 1967 to extend to the local level the national program of historical and cultural preservation, and to survey the town's historical and architectural assets. It oversees the Archival Center, accepts donations of historical material, coordinates research on proposed local historic districts and structures, and offers educational programs to schools and organizations.

Winchester Historical Society, 15 High Street, Winchester, MA 01890. Founded over 50 years ago as a successor to the Winchester Historical and Genealogical Society (1884–1898), which donated many artifacts, documents, photographs, books, and maps that became the basis of the Archival Center collection. The Society sponsors educational activities, public programs, and house tours, and assists in the maintenance of the town's historic resources. It publishes a newsletter on the Society's activities, *The Black Horse Bulletin.*

Donors

Aberjona Nursing Center
Dr. & Mrs. Blaise F. Alfano
All United Realty
American Alarm & Communication/
  Mr. & Mrs. Richard L. Sampson
Eleanor H. & Harry H. Baldwin, 3rd
Bank of Boston
Cynthia Laraway Barone
Barry & McHugh Insurance Agency
Baybank Middlesex
Bixby & Porter Co. Realtors
Ann Blackham & Co., Inc.
Bertha R. & Daniel F. Blanchard
Marjorie Davidson Dyer Blomquist
Bonnell Motors, Inc.
Book Ends/Mildred Cook
Clarence & Margaret Borggaard
Bowman Real Estate/Anne R. Wild
Francis D. Cabour
Calista/Calista Clunan
Cambridgeport Savings Bank
Carlson Real Estate
Century 21 Winchester Realty
Chitel's Men's Shop, Inc.
Christopher Columbus Club, Inc.
Rita Corcoran
Robert J. Costello Funeral Home
Cradock Apothecary, Winchester/Surabian
  Family
Marion G. Crandall
Kenneth F. & Dorothy G. Cullen
The Daisy Shop/Dick Ouellett
Constance Davy
Muriel B. Dawes
Dr. Richard J. DiBella
Dorothea's Florist, Inc.
The Dover Grille
Mr. & Mrs. John H. Driscoll
En Ka
Eye Look Optical
Fells Hardware, Inc.
Cynthia & Albert Fertman
Jay M. Finn Insurance Agency
James J. & Mary E. Fitzgerald
Focus First/Mr. & Mrs. Stephen Lovett
Maurice Freeman

Gateway Travel Service
Marjorie M. Gibson
Jane & Stuart W. Graham
Donna & Gordon Grant
Dorothy F. & Ellis J. Green
Martha & George Hebb
Henderson Stationers, Inc.
Elizabeth C. & Frederick Herberich
Heritage Trail Antiques
The Home Team/William F. Caci, Realtor
Margaret & John Howard
Hunneman & Co. Realtors/Carol F.
  Johnson, Manager
Mrs. James L. Jenks, Jr.
Phyllis H. Johansen
Ralph & Mary Johnson
Victor H. & Suzanne Wadsworth Jonas
Sherman R. & Elinor Josephson
N. Noelle Karp
Kean Flowers
Julie E. & Charles Khuen
Eleanore H. S. Kirk
Trudy Kirkendall
Marie Kennedy & Frances E. Konicek
Margie A. Lamar
Lane Funeral Service, Inc.
Barbara & Alexander Leaf
Lions Club of Winchester
Lombardi Real Estate
Marie Lopinto & John Dacey, Jr.
Lucia Ristorante
M & T Realty Company, Inc./Mr. & Mrs.
  Thomas Derro
Florence & Michael V. MacKenzie
Mahoney's Rocky Ledge/Paul Mahoney
Main Street Optical/Dr. Fred Cohen
Dr. & Mrs. Steven W. Margles
Kenneth A. Mason
Dr. Harley B. Messinger
Arthur G. B. Metcalf Foundation
Andrew M. Monaco
Priscilla Laraway Morse
Mouradian Oriental Rug
Judith & Albert Muggia
Linda & James Naylor
Nook & Cranny Antiques

Norris Funeral Home, Inc.
Dr. Edna D. Parks
John A. Pierce Insurance Agency, Inc.
Jessie & Arthur Pratt
Printwise Gallery/Harvey Kornicks
Celia L. Puffer
Luther W. Puffer, Jr., Inc.
Rita & Charles L. Raffi
Rainbow Shop/Catherine Delaney
Realty World—Winchester Properties
William T. & Beverly Ryerson
Saltmarsh Insurance Agency
Michael D. & Gladys P. Saraco
Nancy Schrock
Scotti & Company, Inc.
Shawmut County Bank NA
Florence & Walter J. Smith
Phyllis M. Stearns
Louise & Charles Stebbins
Swanson Associates Real Estate, Inc./
  Wesley B. Swanson
Sandra M. & Lewis B. Thompson
TSV Video/Rose Tufankjian, Manager
Lillian & Grant Urry
Dorothy Asetine Wadsworth
Waterfield Antiques
Roberta & Gary Watros
George E. Wells
Mrs. Woodford L. Wilcox
W. Allen Wilde & Son Insurance Agency,
  Inc.
Winchester Arts Lottery Council
Winchester Co-operative Bank
Winchester Drug/Alfred P. Caruso
Winchester Hardware
Winchester Landscape & Design
Winchester Ltd. Jewelers
Winchester Optical Shop
Winchester Savings Bank
Winchester Shoe Hospital
Winchester Star
Winchester Travel Advisors
Winchester Wine & Spirits
J. H. Winn, Inc.